The Philosophical Discourses

By

Edward DeLia

The Philosophical Discourses

Copyright ©2026 by Edward DeLia

PRINTED IN THE UNITED STATES OF AMERICA
VIZE PUBLISHING COMPANY
PO BOX 402
NESCONSET, NEW YORK 11767

To Virginia Lowery in Addition to Elias and Virginia Chambart and my uncle Joseph who died fighting against the tyranny of the Third Reich.

Table of Contents

PART ONE

INTRODUCTORY NOTE

An Introductory Note

Being here, sitting here, I think of my benighted past and my ennobled future. In the periphery of existence I am and there I will remain. Yet, that doesn't concern me now. What matters is the truth-the emblem of all things great, the archetype of all hope and ennobled dreams, of metaphysical inquiry and ultimate fulfillment.

These are my last days and I must think of the truth. Even more, I should think of the truth. I doubt that I will continue in green pastures. My past eliminates that hope. Yes, my past! I must think of this too. In order to ascend, I must descend. In order to aspire to the clouds, I must kiss the dirt. True, I did descend during my expired days and in that vomit I now sit. So, shall I ascend during my last benighted evening? Shall a day of flesh be atoned for by an evening of spirit? Shall the fire of my youth be enveloped by the pretended wisdom of advanced age? I shall see. Indeed, I will see.

The ways of my benighted country are dominated by power, lust and greed. As an American, I was as devious as any other. Yet, this means nothing to me now. What concerns me are the great questions-questions which transcend my puny place and time. The great questions embody the ascent of humanity and they are the avenue of my ascension. I care not whether what follows is received well or poorly. Glory is a prize for fools. This contemplation is simply an enfolding of 'my being'.

Edward Delia

May 12, 2014

Chapter 1
Essential Considerations

We cannot presuppose the meaning of philosophy at the beginning of this discourse, yet this does not mean that we cannot recognize philosophical problems when we see them. Meaning and recognition are not twins, but disparate processes.

We can say that philosophers have often expressed an innate desire for truth and wisdom. The initial problem then concerns the meaning and value of these terms. This task, in turn, requires a systematic analysis of the history of philosophy and several other fields of thought. Philosophy does not stand alone, but is in continuous interface with the humanities in addition to the sciences. The foundation of philosophy requires considerable cultural development as its blueprint which when complete will allow a systematic index of the wealth of knowledge to be built upon it.

As it approaches its zenith, philosophy is often a quite serious endeavor. It is concerned with the most significant issues: being-itself, knowledge, beauty, goodness, and divinity. These sacred concerns stand above the mundane concerns of life. It should be noted, however, that the serious need not be the deadly serious. Philosophers have often expressed ideas concerning the nature of humor, laughter, dance, romance and other mundane interests. Thomas Hobbes is a good example with his idea that laughter represents 'sudden glory'. (1) At times, comedy may reveal great insight or wisdom as in the case of Shakespeare's quite comic fictional characters.

Now, it is often easier to recognize what is not than to perceive what is. There are two things philosophy is not. First, philosophy is not a vehicle to render life easier to endure during trivial encounters or to provide maxims to impress the unlearned. Voltaire somewhere said that a witty saying proves nothing. It neither generates profound intellect nor does it render, in most cases, a contribution to the intellectual heritage of mankind. 'What will be will be' or 'everything turns out for the best' are apt examples. One does not even have to be human to believe this. If plants had cognition, that would be their philosophy.

Second, philosophy does not deal with the quantification of variables. Where operational concepts occur science, not philosophy, prevails. Scientific research may influence philosophical conclusions, yet this does not negate the fact that philosophy is distinct from science. Where quantities are discussed by philosophers, as in the case of Kantian categorical analysis, they are analyzed in a general or qualitative manner. (2) By the way, symbolic logic does not provide for the quantification of variables in a scientific manner nor does it provide ways for controlling the factors of internal or external validity. (3) The fact that some philosophers, such as Descartes or Leibniz, have also been great mathematicians or scientists does not negate this truth. Science is one thing, philosophy is another. The two are interrelated, yet not identical.

What philosophy is can be stated in one sentence. Philosophy represents the kingdom of the intellect. This is not a definition, but simply a statement of what the term aspires to. As such, a philosopher must be a master of the kingdom of the intellect. Very few qualify for this distinction and even fewer deserve to be called great philosophers.

Greatness in philosophy depends on three determining criteria. The first is originality or Innovative insight. This criteria is difficult to achieve in totality, but only can be attained by degrees of creative advancement. The reason is that all ideas are influenced by previous thinking. Even Thales, the first recognized Western philosopher, was influenced by previous sources. (4)

The second criteria of greatness is historical influence: that is, influencing the systematic development of the discipline. in Western philosophy, Plato clearly stands above all others in this regard. Whitehead keenly wrote that nearly all philosophy is a series of footnotes to Plato. (5) Aristotle is definitely second in historical influence and possibly was greater during the Middle Ages. The present writer would place Kant third to be followed closely by Descartes. So many others would follow that a detailed list would be unwise and arbitrary.

The third criteria is contemporary interest or the or the power of a philosopher's ideas on the present generation of scholars. This factor is to some degree congruent with, yet not the same as the second. No matter how much influence a philosopher has had in the past, it's the present generation that counts. The potency of his ideas must continue. If his contemporary influence waxes, his historical importance will expand. If his contemporary influence wanes, the unfortunate thinker may be relegated to oblivion.

The contemporary interest in Nietzsche in the 20th Century is an example of the former, the declining interest in the metaphysics of Samuel Alexander in that century illustrates the latter. (6) We are referring here to the waxing and waning of influence over an extended period of time, not a few months or a few years. The exact number of years would be unwise to state. It can be said that no single era can relegate a thinker to oblivion or cause him to ascend to eternal acclaim. Many eras are needed to determine that.

1. Hobbes, Thomas, Leviathan, Revised Edition, eds., A.P. Martinich & Brian Battisdte, Peterbough, ON, Broadview Press, 2010.
2. Luchte, James, Kant's Critique of Pure Reason, Bloomsbury Publishing, 2007
3. Shadish, W., Cook T., Campbell, D., Experimental and Quasi-Experimental Designs for Generalized Causal. Reference, Boston, Haughton Mifflin, 2002.
4. Burnet, John., Early Greek Philosophy, London & Edinburgh, Adam & Charles Black, 1892.
5. Whitehead, Alfred, North, Process and Reality, The Free Press, 1979, pg. 39.
6. Alexander, Samuel, Moral Order and Progress: An Analysis of Ethical Conceptions, 2nd Edition, London, Kegan, Paul, Trench, Trubner & Co., 1891.

Chapter 2
What is Philosophy?

Two Necessary Conditions

There are two necessary, yet not sufficient conditions for the emergence of philosophy. The first is the development of language, the symbolic repository of most known meanings. This condition is necessary both for the coherent phenomenological perception of the world and also for the interpretation of ideas including their precise expression or use in disparate contexts.

The abstract nature of philosophy mandates an advanced medium of language development.

The first historically known approach toward philosophy can be visualized in the 'lament literature' of the Middle Kingdom of Ancient Egypt. (1) It was written by the Egyptian upper-classes and was concerned with the concept of justice, a philosophical concern best examined later by the philosopher Plato. (2) Although Egyptian ideas concerning justice were preliminary, it is obvious that this ancient expression could not occur without the development of an Egyptian sign-picture language which could yield compound propositions.

Other ancient Middle Eastern languages were clearly the vehicle for generating the mythologies of Ancient Babylon or Persia. These myths are not identical with philosophy although they are to some degree congruent with it. The conception of pagan gods or demons, of the origins of the universe and the tragedies of existence, of the divinity of love or the calamity of death, of the fall of kingdoms and the triumph of wickedness, are definitely in no small part a grasping toward philosophy.

In the city-state of Melitos, in ancient Asia Minor around 585 B.C., we arrive at the home of the first recognized Western philosopher, Thales. As stated previously, philosophy is distinct from science due to the fact that philosophy does not usually deal with measurement. Yet, Thales was both a scientist and a sage. He actually predicted an eclipse of the sun- an incredible achievement for a man living in antiquity.

Thales was followed by Anaxamander and Anaximines. The Melesian school of thought which was only a subset of a much wider aggregate of pre-Socratic philosophers, including both Parmenides and Heraclitus, exerted a powerful influence of the history of philosophy. However, this could never have occurred without the existence of the ancient Greek dialects which enveloped and shaped their ideas.

In fact, all philosophers have a similar dependency as all thought is shaped by the grammatical structure or conceptual apparatus of language. Every vernacular embodies a unique thought system which differs from all others and directs or formulates ideas in different ways. This is in part why one language cannot be adequately translated into another, as W. V. O. Quine observed. (3) This means that philosophers using diverse languages are thinking differently which is one reason for distinctive philosophical traditions. Note the difference between English and German philosophy. Of course, there could be other differences such as disparate historical developments or contrasting folkways, yet divergent languages are the main reason.

Without words there can be no perception or thought. All perception is selective perception since pure being can never be seen in its total concreteness. (What we see actually is a phenomenal field decoded through language by an embodied mind.) To glance directly into being as it is, just as it is, would lead to madness. The human mind could not grasp it-it would be too awesome.

This is why we could never see or truly grasp the awesome being of the deity. Our embodied mind would be in shock. Hence, the need for prophets to act as a medium between god and man. Yet, no matter what the issue, words shape and interpret what we see and the mind, within grammatical structure of language, formulates ideas. The human instrument of words allows us to focus in on and identify certain aspects of perception and thereby reduces them to a manageable form. Language also allows us to transcend the here and now by releasing human creativity into unseen symbolic provinces or structures of meaning. As language develops in complexity, so too does the stock of accumulated knowledge.

This raises the question of innate ideas and their relationship to the development of language. Philosophers such as Plato and Leibniz believed in innate ideas and Locke, of course, denied the possibility. Jung advocated that innate ideas were archetypes transmitted genetically from one generation to another. (4) He demonstrated this by a detailed analysis of the content of dreams and mythologies. Jung affirmed that children, for example, report dream images which they could never have experienced, yet which have been recorded in books or manuscripts by distant civilizations. (5) It seems that what is innate is encoded in our genes which then affects the brain and our mentality. In any event, we can only know an idea, whether innate or experienced, through the medium of language.

In addition to the vernacular, there are alternative languages such as mathematics, sign-language or the musical score. Mathematics is a quantitative language or a generalization from elementary or advanced quantifiable relationships. Algebra is in large part a generalization of arithmetic. Natural numbers, imaginary numbers, square roots and more advanced formulations of infinity, functions, probability and game theory among others are necessary for the advancement of insight. It is to be noted that the invention of calculus by Leibniz and Newton was necessary for the development of physics. In the same manner, the recognition of imaginary numbers was a prerequisite for the representation of space-time in Einstein's relativity theory.

Likewise, the notation embodied in the musical score is also an alternative language. Without advanced musical theory the precise meaning of meter, pitch, melody, timbre or mode could not be determined, to say nothing of being put into practice. The musical score itself-notes like C or F-constitute an entire auditory universe, an alternative reality. Upon this, novel instruments can be invented to advance the application of this capacity. It goes without saying that sign-language is also an alternative language and those who employ it differ in their perceptions or thought and live in a divergent symbolic universe.

The emphasis on perception is vital here. It is not true that we see only in a bio-physical manner. This is necessary, yet our impressions are filtered through the structure of the mind which is itself fueled by the lens of language. Language structures not only how we think, but also what we perceive. If a layman examines a slide of human tissue through a microscope, he won't see very much beyond variations of light and impressions he does not understand. Yet, a biologist will observe much more due to the technical concepts learned within his discipline. In this regard, perception and language are the engine of awareness.

Norm Chomsky wrote that the capacity for language in humans is "wired" into our nervous system or biology. (6) The implication of this idea is great. Since philosophers must use language for the expression of their ideas just as everyone else, this means that philosophy must have a biological base. A base that is 'a priori' to all reflection - indeed, a biological 'a priori'. While the biological capacity for language must be molded through the medium of social interaction, this does not negate the ultimate biological base of all thinking. By reduction, the ultimate 'truths' of reflection may stem from are genes, not our minds. Hence, the notion of the 'embodied mind' which was developed by a French thinker is quite relevant here. If our genes do determine our thinking, then rationalists must prepare for the demise of reason since our genes are the sum of an arbitrary, non-rational process of natural selection, not the result of any logical sequence. The door is opened again o faith, intuition and authority.

The Second Necessary Condition

The second necessary condition for the emergence of philosophy is the development of a 'leisure class'. (7) This phrase does not refer to the idle rich engaged in conspicuous consumption. It does designate a category of people who live above the subsistence level and have the time or means to grasp intellectual issues uninhibited by the daily toil for basic survival. This would be realized in a society where there is a surplus of food which in turn is dependent upon a considerable degree of social organization.

Nomads constantly seeking food would have little time for philosophy. It is no accident that the 'lament literature' of the Middle Kingdom of Ancient Egypt emerged in an advanced civilization. The same was true of the city-state of Miletus, the home of Thales. There was a surplus in that city and Thales had the economic freedom to devote himself to higher intellectual endeavors. By the way, there is no implication here that a philosopher must be rich, or more affluent than others, but only that his basic needs be satisfied.

This condition does more, however, than to allow time for philosophy. A higher civilization of the type described above will have an advanced social structure where the status of philosopher will be well-defined and its corresponding role. That status and role will in turn be learned by the next generation through socialization and maintained by a corresponding symbolic universe. In simple nomadic societies, there is no status of philosopher and hence no role. There may be a status of sage, witch doctor or shaman, yet this is not the same as the status of philosopher. Hence, the new generation will not learn of the option of being a philosopher.

It is obvious that there will be no corresponding symbolic universe which will transmit the reality of philosophy's past. In an advanced society, the opposite will occur as the status of philosopher will be well-defined including its corresponding role and universities will maintain that status. Philosophers have the role of teaching and writing books and are paid for their endeavors. That pay is a societal reward and acknowledgement of the value of philosophy. Libraries maintain a history of philosophy and this constitutes a symbolic universe which supports the discipline's reality. Hence, the next generation learns of the status of philosopher and has the option to become one. Philosophy is a product of advanced civilization in addition to being a creator of higher culture. As civilization advances, so too does the conception of philosophy itself. New forms of organization produce new forms of thought. The highest organization is an educational institution which places an emphasis on philosophical research.

The Sensitive Mind

Let it be understood, however, that these two necessary conditions do not in themselves ensure philosophical development. Let it also be understood that these two requirements are social facts. Language is a social fact, as Durkheim demonstrated. (8) In addition, a surplus economy is a social development.

The sufficient conditions cannot be described fully as they are nebulous. Yet, almost certainly one is a powerfully sensitive mind. Sensitive, that is, to the comedy and tragedy of life, to the gap between what is and what ought to be, to the struggles of humanity and the brutality of death or the bland ignorance of the common men who are devoid of philosophical problems. A mind sensitive in its spread and deep in its insight. Such a questioning mind has a biological and psychological realm, but is clearly nurtured in society.

The type of society, its institutions or the nature of its social structure and socialization process profoundly affect the development of this variety of mentality. An agricultural society and a post-industrial economy would obviously nurture a different type of mentality or realm of academic interests. Likewise, the family structure, educational institutions, religious organizations arid political or economic realities also would have a massive affect. Socialization processes are even more vital. Primary socialization during the first years of life creates a 'home' world upon which all else is socially constructed including sub-universes which are later internalized into one's consciousness.

Philosophy rests upon social facts and will later itself become a social fact as reified in books. Philosophy and sociology are divergent disciplines, yet there can be no complete comprehension of philosophy without understanding society. Hence, the importance of a philosophy of sociology.

History is Destiny

History is destiny. There is no greater stupidity than those who wonder about the worth of studying history. Every aspect of this world has a historical vector. You don't study mathematics, you study the history of mathematics. You don't study physics, you study the history of physics. Even the language we speak has a historical vector. We demonstrate the significance of history every time we communicate. Our words are historically conditioned.

Likewise, we are born into a philosophical tradition known as the history of philosophy. This tradition is the base upon which we construct our ideas. Yet, it is often shaped by major historical events. Philosophers writing during the French Revolution would obviously have a different set of ideational priorities than those active during the Old Regime. World War 1 had a massive impact on the development of 20th Century thought. A good illustration would be the intensified interest in Nietzsche's philosophy.

(As an existential affirmation, the present writer was born in 1948, three years after the Atomic Bomb was used on Japan. I recall the 1962 Cuban Missile Crisis in which America and Russia came close to blowing up the world. This event was followed by the war in Vietnam and the Watergate Scandal. These events, not just my study of Hume, Wittgenstein or Whitehead, enveloped or shaped my world-view and those of my generation. Questions were raised about the destiny of man, of society and of god. Yet, somehow we went on. Many retained their idealism and hope of making this a better world. So far from fear, so close to death, hail to you the first post-Hiroshima generation.)

The Primacy of Wonder

The experience of wonder is often thought to be a prerequisite for philosophy. Whitehead believed that philosophy begins and ends in wonder. (9) Other great philosophers have made similar judgments. Yet, there are problems with this belief. What exactly is wonder? In a sense, it is more of an emotional rather than a rational experience. To some degree, it is related to ignorance.

We understand little of the cosmos and have a sense of awe or wonder at its seeming majesty. A finite being must always exist in a state of relative ignorance or wonder while an infinite mind, if one exists, would never experience wonder, but rather total comprehension. Wonder is a human emotion, perhaps shared by the higher primates. A great ape, in stark ignorance of what surrounds him, might feel some rudimentary sense of wonder.

In any case, a sense of wonder is not specific as a stimulus to philosophy. It has also motivated poets, scientists, artists and prophets. Einstein described the significance of wonder in stimulating scientific inquiry. (10) Otto discusses the element of fascination in the awareness of the divine. (11) Shelly's poem, *To A Skylark*, provokes a sense of wonder and insight. (12) Turner's painting, *Dido Building Carthage*, combines creative imagination, classical mythology and unending fascination for both historian and art patron. (13) Clearly, wonder is not specific to philosophy.

The Experience of Evil

Schopenhauer maintained that evil seems to be a necessary ingredient of life, not just a chance event or a singular misfortune. (14) Evil presents a problem, a problem which may not rise to the level of philosophical examination, yet has a tendency to do so in great minds. It is one of the keys to philosophical awareness, not a necessary one, yet still a key. Analytic philosophers generally ignore the problem of evil while wisdom philosophers have never stopped discussing its importance.

On an individual level, there is frustration, suffering, death and the shock of non-being. On a social level, there is slavery, racism, war, corruption and colonial exploitation. On an organic level, there is the suffering of animals, the waste in evolutionary development, not to mention limited life spans, limited foresight, limited cognitive ability, limited power and limited emotional empathy. On a theological level, there is the anomie concerning the existence or non-existence of god, the hostility of a seemingly hostile universe and the fear that our lives are headed toward calamity. The big question of evil is its mere existence. (15) In Biblical terms, evil must have existed before the fall of man since the mythological first parents had limited foresight which led to the original sin. The mere existence of evil is a hole into which all joy must be drained. It is a shield against human fulfillment. Evil seems to make everything that should be, not be. Every aspect of reality seems to be enveloped by evil intent.

The big question is this. Does the reality of evil negate the existence of an all-good, all-powerful god?

A question which we will later attempt to answer.

Truth and Wisdom

Truth and wisdom are philosophy's highest law. They provide order and direction to the discipline. They are also the highest aim of civilized man. They express what philosophers ultimately cherish. Plato asserted that all philosophers are motivated by the quest for wisdom or truth. (16) Spinoza, Berkeley, Schopenhauer and others have made similar statements.

It should be noted that Plato believed that the love of wisdom or truth is evident only in philosopher-kings which gives them the right to govern. Others are motivated by the desire for personal gain or glory. (17) Many philosophers believe that they are superior to others based on their advanced intellect. This is a grave error.

(The greatest minds that I have ever known as teachers, Paul Edwards and William McEwen, did not believe they were superior. Both were open, sociable and brilliant in their insights. They believed that students were both equal and unequal. Equal in the sense that all people have feelings of worth and dignity. Not equal in the sense that students obviously did not do an equal amount of research as they did in the field of philosophy. I have attempted to emulate their example. I could say of both of them what is expressed in a famous line spoken by Hamlet. To phrase it in more updated English, I would say that they were as men as just as any that I have met or have had conversation with. (Hamlet 3.2.44.) The notion of superiority or the earned right to dominate were unknown to them.)

Plato seems to ignore the fact that all men are subject to higher and lower passions. The greatest mind, as Schopenhauer observed, often possesses some mundane urge or defect which connects him with the common base of mankind. (18) In reverse, the most ordinary citizen often expresses noble dreams about the perplexing issues of existence.

The difference is one of degree, not quality. Philosophers exhibit a love of wisdom or truth to a greater degree than most other men. This does not qualify them, however, for special honors or the right to govern. Wise men are not always moral and a rigid classification of men often leads to a closed society, as Popper argued. (19)

(Of course, Plato had a rigid type of training and education which he believed would generate a utopian society. Whether he thought this type of society could actually be achieved is a matter for intellectual debate. What is relevant, however, is that utopias often have a hard time adjusting to the frictions of reality. To exclude a large segment of mankind from government is unwise, no matter what sort of method is used to determine the question of who will govern. As Lincoln stated, the Declaration of Independence declares that all men are created equal, including men of limited intelligence and prospects. (20) They are entitled to the same opportunities and chance for governance as any other.

This may not lead to a perfect society, yet nothing is perfect, only actual.)

Did Philosophy Arise from the 'A Priori'?

Did philosophy arise from the 'a priori' desire for wisdom or truth? At first, this question seems quite easy to answer, but on a deeper analysis serious problems arise. In surveying the surviving fragments of the Ancient Greek philosophers, there is little doubt that they possessed an 'a priori' desire for wisdom and truth. Pythagoras states that a philosophical life is one dedicated to the attainment of truth. (21) Plato described Socrates as a citizen of Athens whose life embodied. the quest for truth. Bishop Berkeley described philosophy as the study of wisdom and truth. (22) Descartes and Spinoza advocated the same idea.

Yet, perhaps there are deeper considerations here. Nietzsche questioned the value of wisdom or truth and denied that this 'a priori' desire is the ultimate reason behind the quest to philosophize. (23) He believed that falsehood is more valuable than truth. Machievelli, of course, is credited with recognizing the utility of deception in statecraft. (24) Plato himself suggested the 'noble lie' as a legitimation of his ideal society. (25) Goffman advised that a life dedicated to honesty or truth could be debilitating to one's social existence. (26) In fact, lying and deception may be the fabric which holds society together. But, there is more here, much more. Nietzsche questioned Socrates' motivations. He described Socrates as an ugly man, inside and out, an outsider who used philosophy as a blade to strike back at society. (27) Truth was not his quest, but harm. Philosophy was a blade in his hand to cut and slash at those who rejected him. It must be remembered, as Kenneth Harl has written, that the younger Socrates was a hoplite warrior who engaged in fierce action in combat during the Second Peloponnesian War. (28) A hoplite was a powerful figure and held a weapon which could decapitate an enemy in battle. Very few Athenians had the stamina to become hoplites and that is the reason these warriors had special duties within the state power structure. This is quite a different Socrates than the one presented by Plato.

The reason for this disparity is that all roles have both a front and a back region. (29) The front region displays the desired impression; the back region contains everything that is hidden. Plato's Socrates may only be the result of a front region impression: namely, the impression Socrates conveyed to Plato as a kindly older man. Other aspects of Socrates' life were hidden from his admiring student.

Freud has written of unconscious urges determining rational thought. (30) Mannheim has revealed that much thought is either a rejection or justification of mundane social interests. (31) This idea can be clearly seen in Marxist utopian writings or Christian attempts to prove by logic the existence of god. Metaphysical speculations concerning a perfect world could have their root in a deep-seated hatred of the existing world.

What can we discern from all this? Clearly, in light of an objective historical analysis, there is evidence in the writings of philosophers of a profound interest in truth and wisdom. This is their stated concern. We have noted, however, that some thinkers have questioned the value of truth and we must keep in mind that one's stated motives might not be the real ones. In some cases, philosophy could be an attempt to heap revenge on a hostile social order or a veneer to give conviction to one's wishful dreams of order or goodness. The truth may be hidden in the recesses of our unconscious.

Is Truth or Wisdom Attainable?

Is it possible for a finite mind to discern the nature of truth and exhibit wisdom? Socrates believed. it was and developed a method of determining the criteria of truth by establishing universal definitions. (32) The quest for universal abstractions was the key to the 'Socratic Method' and his entire mission was embodied in this quest. Socrates, as interpreted by Plato, did realize that one word could symbolize different facts, yet his ideal was the universal meaning revealed by the word. This quest must reluctantly be regarded as a failure.

All definitions are expressed in language and all languages present only a selective perception of reality. (33) The total reality of being is never reachable. Only minute fragments or selective formats of the totality are reachable as determined by the words and grammar of any specific vernacular. We do not react directly to physical or social realities, but rather to the concepts describing them.

This means that language is a thought system and not one of these thought systems is equivalent to any other despite some congruencies. In this respect, it makes little difference what the thought system is. It may be the vernacular, but also mathematics, geometry, sign language, scientific notation, the musical score or even symbolic forms of art. They all have one thing in common: namely, they control the content and direction of thought. This is what Heidegger meant when he asserted that art not merely is part of culture, but also creates culture in itself. (34) We are all prisoners of the limits and structure of our languages.

Every language has a history, a shape, a contour and a destiny. The English language at this reading is not exactly the same as it was during the time of Shakespeare. Languages evolve through changes in culture, as it creates culture itself, as often mandated by pragmatic modifications.

If we regress into the past, English is unrecognizable and resembles German from whose language family it derives. The same is true of all other vernaculars including the ancient Greek languages during the life time of Socrates.

What exactly does this amount to? In short, philosophers using different languages are often thinking differently, defining terms differently as well as positing divergent unit assumptions.

There can never be a final universal philosophy or a universal definition of goodness or truth or justice or of anything else for that matter.. Even the assertions above would not hold universally in other thought systems. Given his limited comprehension of language, Socrates sought to develop universal meanings.

If he could have visualized the historical development of diverse language families in their total complexity, he might not have attempted so naïve an enterprise.

Linguists estimate that there are over six thousand languages, not to mention numerous dialects or language families. To repeat, Quine has demonstrated that one language cannot be adequately translated into another. (35)

The interconnections between words in different languages is based on little more than conventional assumptions and outward references as interpreted by translators. In all the vernaculars, there is a mixture of words and grammars that are endless in their permutations and combinations. Thus, the Socratic goal of universal definitions is little more than a futile Socratic dream.

Process Philosophy

Heraclitus described the world as fire, constantly changing and never static. (36) It is as a planet spinning off into the cosmos always subject to modification. What is today will never be tomorrow! Change or process is the key. Being is experienced through becoming. In the personal realm, every day presents something novel.

There may be similar patterns at times, yet nothing is exactly the same. Some things change so slowly that the transition may not be immediately recognizable. Other changes occur more rapidly, yet nothing is static. This is why the past cannot be recaptured, but only recalled with nostalgia, regret or indifference. Recalled, that is, or modified through the lens of the present. (37) During the twentieth century, this conception of process was most fully developed by Whitehead. (38)

Process is also relevant in the realm of ideas and is the key to all symbolic meanings. All ideas may change in time. This is not only true of ideas in the humanities or social sciences, but also of ideas in the physical sciences or mathematics or for that matter in everyday experience. Process or change is the key to understanding the meaning of meaning.

Let us begin by examining the ideas postulated in physics which is the most developed of the natural sciences. The idea of patterned relationships in nature was most fully developed in antiquity by the Greeks. (39) All scientists are indebted to them in regard to the conception of natural law. We are all students of ancient Greek civilization. Yet, the assumptions posited by the idea of natural law has to this day never be fully examined although there have been numerous attempts.

As an illustration, Newton's laws of motion have been regarded as being quite accurate as applied to the realm of mechanical motion. In fact, they are quite accurate as determined by measurements. That is, during the present cosmic era. The universe has existed for billions of years and the accuracy of Newton's laws now mandates nothing about their potency in the mechanical realm hundreds of thousands or millions of years from now.

These laws, as all laws of physics, are not universally true, but rather only pertain to limited domains. Even at present, Newton's laws of motion cannot be applied to quantum or electrical phenomena. The same is true of the general or specific theories of relativity which are not applicable within the domain of black holes. (40) No universal field theory in physics has ever been widely accepted as new ideas are being expounded every day.

It cannot be eliminated that the operations of nature may change over time. Epistemology does not mandate ontology. The operations of nature are not inhibited by our conceptions of them. We see only a phenomenal field as interpreted by an embodied mind. Yet, new patterns or arrangements may be spontaneously generated. (The present author does not agree with the conventional wisdom in phenomenology that phenomena cannot be regarded as being 'out there' or 'in here' or that they simply exist in themselves).

We see phenomena as per our symbols and interpret them. In our interpretation, we impose the cognitive patterns of the mind upon phenomena. Yet, it is possible to assume, as Kant does, that there is a noumenon or an 'out there' behind phenomena which we may never understand. (41) Behind phenomena, of course, only as a metaphor, yet enough of a metaphor to free us form the mistaken notion that our interpretation of law mandates the ontology of being.

Mathematics and Geometry

The constructs of pure mathematics or geometry are no different since they have limited applicability and are valid only by means of undefined assumptions, defined terms, postulates or extensions of these as derived at by the proper exercise of deductive logic. Mathematical constructions cannot be applied beyond the specific domain of operations under consideration. Applied mathematics is simply an arbitrary application of mathematical constructs to limited domains which often become irrelevant when applied to other realms of discourse.

This is also true of absolute numerical values which are absolute only within a specific domain of meaning. Kurt Godel has proven that the consistency of any mathematical system cannot be proven within the system itself. (42) If the system is consistent, it cannot be complete. Completeness and consistency cannot subsist within the same system.

(The whole idea of a comprehensive logical system, both consistent and complete, stems from the mistaken belief, derived from Plato, that mathematical or logical constructs have an independent reality or ontological status. That they subsist somewhere and have a being all their own which we can discover in an 'a priori' manner. The truth is that they are the arbitrary constructs of the human mentality.)

As concerning the question of applicability, let us examine the discipline of geometry. There are Euclidean and non-Euclidean geometries which are all internally valid, but which generate divergent conclusions. in Euclidean geometry, as an example, parallel lines are extended indefinitely and never intersect. (43) In Riemann's geometry, there are no parallel lines. (44) Thus, all geometries are based on different unit assumptions, definitions, postulates and extensions of these considerations.

The question of which geometry is descriptive of the observed universe cannot be proven within any one of these specific systems. This is an empirical matter relating to precise observations which are themselves subject to the process of modification. Kant believed that Euclidean geometry is descriptive of phenomena; Einstein used non-Euclidean assumptions. These attempts to apply geometry to the universe were arbitrary and could only relate to specific realms of discourse despite their sporadic predictive capacity. We are beyond the edge of certainty here.

The Facts and Theories of History

The same is true of the so-called facts and theories of history. They are true only within the bounds of specific realms of meaning arid are no more than probable. In most cases, a low degree of probability is the best that can be achieved. Absolute laws in history are impossible since all historical formats relate only to specific cultures or social structures. Karl Popper has written adroitly on the futility of establishing universal historical laws. (45)

Jean Lyotard has demonstrated the debilitating aspects of meta-narratives in both literature and history. (46) No historical situation has ever been repeated in full detail. Insights can be derived from studying history, yet they cannot be generalized to other formats. When they are so applied, grave errors often occur. Every era has to be studied within the realm of its singular historical context.

There is no greater absurdity than those who assert that history has demonstrated something. History has not demonstrated anything. Historians are the only ones who attempted - in most cases unsuccessfully - to establish historical patterns. New theories are constantly overturning older generalizations as the continuing process of research is revealed. The so-called 'hard' facts of history are not as 'hard' as some believe. A fact is an ordering of reality in terms of a theoretical interest. (47) All historical facts are based on the viability of historical sources and these sources often disagree. Moreover, newly found sources, may overturn older ones. As an example, epigraphy or the study of ancient inscriptions has generated new insights relating to the Second Peloponnesian War (48).

Some older facts have turned out not to be facts at all. Adolf Hitler was supposed to have died from a self-inflicted gunshot wound to his brain. The Russians later presented evidence that he might have poisoned himself. Some historians have combined, the two methods of death: namely, that he took poison a moment before he shot himself. The real truth may never be known. What exactly are the facts here?

History is only as good as its sources and all documents are not equal. In order to have rational faith in historical sources, they should at a minimum be consistent with other sources and stem from a reliable person, agency or other institution. Of course, what is reliable is a matter of interpretation and disagreements are common. Except for very simple statements relating to names and dates of occurrence, the so-called facts of history have to be regarded as no more than extremely limited probability assertions.

As an illustration, it is generally accepted that John Kennedy was assassinated on November 22, 1963. The sources are extensive in support of this assertion, but it would be wrong to regard this as an absolutely true statement. Islamic cultures use a different calendar dating back to the days of Mohammad and they would record a different date as would the Chinese given their divergent calendar.

In Tokyo, it was past midnight when Kennedy died and the date there would be recorded November 23, 1963. Moreover, in the remote future, documents that are now available may be lost and doubt might be generated on that basis. Are we absolutely sure when Cyrus the Great was born or when Darius II died? These would be obvious facts during their eras, but are much less obvious today. The answer would depend on your rational faith in ancient sources. Reliable sources are the ontology of history.

Uncertainty is even more obvious when one examines motives or causes in history. Hume somewhere wrote that history only happens once. Hence, there can be no testing or experimental analysis of the factors relating to internal or external validity.

Given this limitation, historians still try to be objective and for a good part they are, yet a certain amount of fiction can be found in the pages of any history to fill in the gaps where sources are absent or irrelevant to the determination of causes or motives. Since everything we know has a historical vector, all of human culture must in part be fictional. Mythology is in large part overt fiction; other aspects of culture are definitely covert in this capacity.

Sociology and Psychology

The same is true of the other major social sciences, sociology and psychology. At most, they offer moderate to high degrees of probability and their conclusions are definitely devoid of certainty.

Controlled experimentation in social science aims at attaining internal or external validity and reliability, yet often fails to achieve this goal due to the complexity of the human organism among other issues. Surveys are accurate within a certain degree of probability, but the samples are often small and non-representative of the entire population. Statistical analysis is obviously no more than probable by its very nature and cannot relate to every individual condition. Participant observation and psychoanalysis have their uses, yet any conclusions derived from their application may rarely be generalized into a wider context. Testing and reexamination are always required. Max Weber observed that those who desire to achieve a final theory are looking through a glass in the dark. Robert Merton wisely wrote that social-scientific theories are only 'theories of the middle range', (49) No scientific theory, social-scientific or natural scientific explains all the facts in its domain. (50)

Logic and Artificial Certainty

There is no certainty in logic. All logical sequences relate only to specific formats outside of which they are impotent. Some intellectuals claim that A=A is a certain proposition, yet it is possible to generate doubt here.

The statement relates to a specific symbolic universe of meaning in which the symbol is interpreted as designating an equality of values. There is no universal necessity in this designation as this symbol could be defined differently in another domain. In a contrary domain, A would not equal A.

Those who advocate that this 'a priori' statement or tautology is true in its limited domain are simply champions of the obvious as this is not denied here. It is not even denied that a tautology may have uses, a significant tautology.

As Richard III would say, "Richard loves Richard, that is, I am I". There is an inner delight in this artificial certainty or identification of being with being. in Heidegger's terms, being is itself. A rose is a rose was Gertrude Stein's insight. Rich in vision, yet devoid of revealing anything about the external world. What is denied is that there is any absolute certainty in logical statements in the sense that they can be extended beyond themselves to diverse realms of discourse. Absolute certainty is artificially created by humans.

The Order of Nature Problem

This quest for certainty can be seen in the 'order of nature' problem which has dominated thinking over the centuries. How can we be sure that the laws which were operational in the past will continue into the future? Hume correctly demonstrated that this problem cannot be solved either by 'a priori' or empirical argumentation. (51) Yet, this great thinker ignores an important vector of the problem: namely, there is no reason in the first place to expect the future to resemble the past.

Process is universal and the 'laws of nature' will be modified over time. Lay people speak of the 'laws of nature' as if they are static and unchangeable. In truth, they have limited applicability within specific symbolic universes which are constantly being modified. Epistemology does not mandate ontology. The universe does not have to abide by human expectations. Shelley expressed this idea as follows.

We are as clouds that veil the midnight moon;

How restlessly they speed, and gleam, and quiver,

Streaking the darkness radiantly,

Yet, soon Night comes round

And they are lost forever...

Man's yesterday may ne'er be like his morrow,

Naught may endure, but Mutability.

Shelley's talent for poetic truth must be admired. His poetic vision was great: ideal, abstract and keen. (52)

Process and the Structure of Reason

Everything changes including the structure of reason itself. As in the case of the 'laws of nature', reason itself is in process. The idea that reason is static or fixed is a misconception. As life in the universe evolves over vast cosmic periods, novel ontological regularities will be generated which will affect human mentality.

As Jung demonstrated, the mind is not exempt from the evolutionary process. (53) As the mind evolves, the structure of reason will be modified. Of course, the mind evolves in functional relation to the vast organic processes determining the structure of the brain.

In an unreflective manner, we often speak of 'proper' logic or 'proper' scientific procedure. Yet, there is an important question to be asked here: namely, 'proper' to whom? 'Proper' to singular individuals, to government agencies, to experts or to the consensus of mankind in general. Any specific answer would be arbitrary. What is 'proper' to me may not be 'proper' to you. Also, what is 'proper' during one era in history or in one culture may not be 'proper' in another. Most philosophers with their bias toward intellectualism would answer 'proper' to experts. The problem is that experts often disagree as to what 'proper' logic is or even what 'proper' scientific method constitutes. (54)

(Before proceeding further, let it be understood that the present author has been greatly influenced by process philosophy in addition to his conviction that our embodied minds perceive only phenomena. Evolution is simply one vast generalization in biology which has a great deal of empirical evidence to support it. Yet, the basic ideas presented here that all life is in process rests upon metaphysical grounds included in writings of Heraclitus, Whitehead and McEwen.

The theory of evolution is merely a modern scientific way of expressing what was originally a metaphysical insight. All scientific theories, no matter how vast or empirically verified, are capable of disproof. Yet, even if this should occur which is unlikely, the basic belief that all life is in process would still remain unshaken. By the way, when the words 'universe' or 'world' are used rather than phenomena, this is just employed as a metaphor for purposes of literary variation. These words are meant to refer properly to phenomena.)

Wat is considered 'proper' is simply a function of the mental development of our species at the present stage of evolution. As the brain evolves, the mind and all cognitive development will be modified. (55) During distant epochs, random mutations and other evolutionary modifications might restructure the human brain generating novel epistemological apperceptions or cognitive capacities. In turn, these cognitive capacities might result in a mental enhancement the product of which would render contemporary wisdom to be mere foolishness.

Even at present, the categories underlying human reason cannot be demonstrated. These are strains in the structure of reason itself. The so-called law of contradiction cannot be proven by mathematical, logical or any other means. Any attempt to prove it would assume the 'law of contradiction' in its sequence of argumentation. You would be assuming what you intend to proye.

The same is true of the so-called law of causality. Hume's famous analysis of causation clearly demonstrates this: namely, that there is no power or necessary connection between cause and effect. (56) Yet, on a deeper level, any attempt to prove the 'law of causality' must assume this category of order within its interpretative sequence. The human mind is hopelessly governed by principles of interpretation which cannot be proven.

(The basic problem here is that all phenomena are interpreted by an embodied mind. That is, a mind deeply influenced by the human biological organism. Emerging from obscure conditions, this mind seems to be directed toward trying to understand the origin of circumstances. Where did this world come from?

Why is there something rather than nothing? These problems are evoked by the epistemological operations of the human mind as interpreted by symbols. Epistemology does not mandate ontology. Simply because we think phenomena must have a cause or that there must be some origin to circumstances does not mean that the ontological regularities must obey our expectations. That something should exist rather than nothing is no more absurd than the belief that nothing should exist rather than something. In this human world, our epistemological posits have a limited utility. Yet, in general, they produce obstacles in the path of wisdom.)

A.J. Ayer has argued that the unproven nature of the categories of interpretation is not significant either for science or for human discourse in general. (57) The progress of science, he contends, is not endangered by the fact that some philosophers continue to be puzzled by the problem of induction. To the contrary, science is justified by its pragmatic value: namely, it works or is conductive to future research and regular predictive capacity.

While this view is correct to a certain extent, the extent is not unlimited. It cannot be assumed that external success implies internal correctness. Inadequate theories have often had a limited predictive capacity that was later proven to be bogus. Even if the predictive value is extensive, it would not imply, as we have seen, that it could be applied to divergent realms of discourse. Despite what Ayer believes, profound metaphysical queries still remain unanswered.

Most of what is regarded as 'proper' logic has been formulated by Aristotle. (58) His ideas, however, have been modified greatly after 1945. Philosophers have regarded 'proper' logic as the battleground of adulthood. Yet, the term 'proper' is arbitrary, relative to specific contexts, objective only to a limited extent and it is often nebulous.

The main contention here is that what is regarded as 'proper', 'proper' logic or 'proper' behavior, ultimately rests on one's concrete existence, an existence which has both individual and collective vectors. Philosophy is a dialogue to oneself or a private note to the collectivity. It is an extension of one's biography. (59)

The Prime Existential Choice- Reason, Faith, Authority or Intuition

Freud demonstrated that reason is often influenced by unconscious motivations and desires. (60) Jung described an integrated self composed of consciousness, the personal unconscious and the collective unconscious. (61) A critique of pure reason must include a critique of pure irrationality.

Reason is not as pure as it seems. It is often mixed with sexual desire, the will to power, the urge for destruction, the omnipresence of sin and the burden of anxiety. Reason is extremely weak and is often incapable of solving metaphysical queries especially in regard to the doctrine of final ends. Once again, it cannot establish universal definitions of wisdom, of truth, of beauty, of goodness or for that matter of any other vital concept.

Attempts to establish a universal logic have failed. Artificial certainty and logical games cannot answer the fundamental question of the meaning of meaning.

Every serious scholar in biology, psychology, neurology or anthropology has been awed by the brain's complexity. It is clearly an evolutionary development derived from less complex brain structures.

There is a wide gap between the mentality of lower primates and human mentality. Our capacity for what we call reason and memory is enormous. But, as the brain evolves over millions of years, this implies that there could be a wide gap between our present mentality and the cognitive capacity of our distant progeny. They might regard us as a fallen species, quite underdeveloped.

In its most essential form, the human brain is a 'processing unit'- an organic one at that- as are the brains of our earlier primates. As the brain evolves, emergent qualities will become apparent and operational. In general, organic development from the simple to complex induces emergence.

The evolutionary trail of organic advancement suggests that emergence leads to novel forms of adaptation which are not only physical, but mental since the mind evolves with the body or more specifically in functional relation with the brain. (62) As an illustration, one-celled organisms exhibit elementary forms of attraction or aversion. Plants exhibit more advanced reactions in the form of positive or negative tropisms. Lower primates often possess a keen capacity for sight, sound or smell. Humans obviously have higher mental capacities.

Thus, reason is no more than a survival tool of a 'processing unit, an arbitrary adaptation, which we refer to as the brain. All of our logical sequences may merely be a juncture, a cognitive cog, which is referred to as a reasonable judgment. Yet, this reasonableness, in the end, is only a consequence of an internal process which is both groundless and without substance. What is often called an insight is really only an empty illumination or an arbitrary output of a 'processing unit' which may not be capable of generating truth or wisdom.

During the formation of a judgment, a juncture of reasonableness is reached, a stopping point, which we shall be refer to as a cognitive cog. This stopping point determines what is reasonable in metaphysics, in ethics, in politics or in any other human endeavor. But, this reasonableness is based on a groundless system of posited criteria which may have a limited or sporadic pragmatic value, yet is no more than an adaptation or the resultant of an arbitrary and irrational evolutionary process of whose origin we are unaware.

Reason is not a universal illumination, a 'logos' or a guide to history. It is no more than an empty illumination, an illumination whose judgments are never final. The judgments of reason are punctured by nebulous and unending contradictions. No judgment is as simple as one, two or three. Six plus four equals ten on a base ten system. In another base, the sum would be different. One, two or three- this is arithmetic, not ontology.

An overconfidence in reason leads to enormous errors including an indifference to other sources of knowledge such as experience, emotional intelligence, intuition or spirituality. Logic alone cannot explain the entirely of human existence. In addition, reason is not entirely good. If there is any doubt about this, consider the consequences of the evil genius of Adolf Hitler.

Reason has its utility and there is no attempt to deny this here. Within specific contexts, reason or logic can generate a limited wisdom.

The problem is that these insights can rarely be generalized beyond the symbolic universe in which they arose and even within their native symbolic universe modifications are often necessary. In the end, there is no final truth or wisdom. What is conceived as wisdom or truth today may be regarded as foolishness to our distant progeny. They may have different ideas as to what is reasonable.

There are other sources of knowledge and a profound understanding of those alternative sources night open the way to a deep wisdom unknown to us today. Experience is often a guide to action, intuition reveals to us intimations of what is true despite our lack of insight as to its origin, authority is quite necessary during the complex process of socialization and spirituality seems essential when being confronted with the finality of death.

Objections to these Conclusions

There are several major objections to the conclusions presented above which should be responded to. First, it is argued that the faculty of reason has generated massive advances in Western civilization in the fields of physics, chemistry, medicine engineering, space flight, computers, business, art, music and numerous other enterprises too exhaustive to mention here. Is it sensible to undermine a faculty which has generated such noble advances? Moreover, has any other source of knowledge generated an equal number of achievements?

The answer to the first question is that there is no attempt here to undermine the faculty of reason or its achievements. The technical advances of reason are what they are and remain what they are. What is being asserted here is that human judgments are limited in application to specific symbolic universes or contexts and may be modified in the future.

Ontologically, there is no 'a priori' reason to expect the future to resemble the past. We do so only because our epistemological inclinations are directed toward determining the origin of circumstances. Yet, this is simply an 'a posteriori' inclination and in no manner does it inhibit spontaneous ontological modifications of which we are unaware due to their emergence from obscure origins.

The brain itself may be governed by principles which the mind may never comprehend. The organic nature of the brain determines out thinking. As that organic structure is modified over vast time periods, so too will our thinking be modified. Aristotle might then be regarded in the same manner as we today regard Paleolithic man. Everything we regard as sound scientific principle might then be overthrown. Novel and profound ideas of science may find themselves in the dust bowl of history. Man may be transcended by a new race with superior endowments.

Change the organic structure of the brain and human mentality will be modified. Richard Taylor made an interesting suggestion in this regard which is relevant here. (63) Humans often have highly developed memories and poorly developed precognition. Memory is functionally connected with various parts of the brain which no doubt give rise to this capacity. Lower organisms often possess more intense precognition and are quite aware of impending disasters before they occur. Let's imagine a situation where men had poorly developed memories and highly developed precognition.

If this were the case, the whole notion of voluntary action, ethical choice or causal necessity would be altered or even negated. It might even change our ideas about death or destiny to say nothing of history or science assuming that those considerations or disciplines were possible in such a hypothetical situation.

Those who champion the universality of science forget about the infinite myriads of space and time. There seems to be no limit to this universe of billions of light years the bulk of which is completely unexplored. It is arrogance to state that the scientific generalities operational here at this stage of evolution must apply to the totality of the phenomenal field in all remote regions of space.

Time itself is essentially an ontological progression despite the fact that it may be scientifically measured in many ways. The infinity of time shall wipe out everything including our primitive ideas of science. Einstein stated that power is here and now while an equation is forever. He was wrong. Both are here and now.

Reason in Philosophy

How important is reason in philosophy? It is obvious that all philosophers rely upon reason during their research. Yet, is doubtful that reason or logic alone could be the foundation stone of philosophy. Reason is a much more expansive concept than logic and a philosopher may decide to negate the relevance of logic in human affairs. To some extent, the existentialists did precisely this. (64)

Our rational capacity is broad and subsists in functional relation with our conscious, unconscious and emotional capacities including our bodily responses. Thus, what is called reasonable is to some degree a bodily response which should be investigated by a future generation of behaviorists.

Dreams have been defined by psychologists as an alternative thought process. (65) While there are differences concerning dream interpretation, it is obvious that there is a symbolic form of meaning discernible here as described in the work of Freud, Adler, Jung and others. (66) The wisdom, conveyed in dreams may have profound significance not only in personal relationships, but also in solving intellectual problems as in the case of the dream which inspired the genesis of the periodic table in chemistry. (67)

The body may at times emit meaningless stimuli as an ultimate brute fact. Yet, dreams must be regarded as more than detached memories evoked by a sleeping brain. It cannot be overemphasized that all reasoning is embodied. We are a 'lived body'. (68) Everything that we are, think or feel are contained within the body and its physical or chemical functioning. This is not a reductionism, but simply a matter of fact. A truth we desire to deny. Our destiny is our body. Our reason goes only as far as our anatomy. A different type of brain would yield a different type of rationality.

Herein lies an answer to the second question ventured previously concerning whether any other source of knowledge has also produced a record of achievement equal to that of our rational capacity. The truth is that reason did not achieve what it did in isolation, but was rather mixed with other sources of knowledge without which it would be barren. Logic alone would lead us into the most intense absurdities. Anchored in the body, in emotion, in lived experience and under the control of authority, reason is more solidly directed and functionally motivated. Intuition, faith and precognition (which biologists call anticipation) are also vital here. Kant himself wrote that both logic and experience are both necessary in forming judgments. (69) Anselm believed that all reason must be grounded in faith and authority. (70)

Faith binds us into a personal relationship to the truth. Authority directs our access to the wisdom of the past by teachers who convey the great ideas of philosophy. Total freedom devoid of authority would lead us into a hell where there is no reason. Reason is developmental and needs the discipline of authority to direct it.

There is no substitute for teachers who impose rigorous demands on students. The citadel of reason is grounded in the non-rational.

It should also be noted that reason develops in a dialectical relationship with society. (71)

What constitutes 'reasonableness' to an upper-class Jewish intellectual in New York City would not necessarily be 'reasonable' to a peasant in Haiti. Standards of judgment or what is vaguely called common sense would be different. If the upper-class Jewish intellectual experienced anxiety, she might think it 'reasonable' to see a psychologist. Yet, the peasant might feel emotionally upset, yet not know of anxiety is. The problem might be interpreted as caused by a curse which must be removed. The dialectics of society cannot be ignored.

The Emotions

Philosophers often do not acknowledge the importance of the emotions in philosophical deliberations. What is an emotion? Spinoza defined an emotion as a modification of the body in which bodily activity is either increased or diminished and the ideas thereof. (72) Some psychologists believe emotions are related to reason in that emotions inform us as to what is harmful or beneficial to our being. (73) In any case, our emotions can define our true being as powerfully as any rational deliberation. Any singular philosophy is a product not only of reason, but also of the emotional make-up of the thinker. The ideas of other disciplines are equally so determined.

A purely detached, entirely rational demeanor has never been achieved by any philosopher, not even Descartes or Spinoza. This is a false ideal and an enormous deception. Man is a creature of bone and flesh, of emotions as well as reason. Philosophers are often driven by non-rational motivations and their overall world view is shaped by them. These non-rational motivations are derived from the social-psychological realm and include sexual desires, urges to achieve greatness or motivations leading to destruction. What a philosopher finds interesting is often not determined by rational considerations, but rather by social-psychological ones. We don't know why we are interested in something, yet we are. The cause may lie outside the realm of reason since many ideas may have their roots in our basic instincts.

Despite what Max Weber believed, there is no such thing as value-free science. (74) The inclusion of values in research may be minimized, yet never eliminated. Machines do not write philosophy. This is achieved by creatures of bone and flesh who envelop values. What topic to write about, what procedure to utilize, what type of knowledge to aspire to and how to develop that knowledge will never be entirely determined by reason.

Temperament, demeanor, character, personality, emotional make-up or our entire animal functioning will in addition to reason be the key to one's philosophy. The philosophy is me; *La philosophie est moi*. In any language, biography is the key to philosophy. Many philosophers love to hide their link to humanity in order to render a false impression: namely, that some great force speaks through them such as destiny or a spirit of the age. The truth is that they eat, drink or urinate in the same manner as the common bloke and they also sit upon nothing more than their own behind.

The Genetic Fallacy

The genetic fallacy states that the factors involved in the genesis of ideas do not affect their validity or truth. Yet, this genetic fallacy is quite limited in its, application. In terms of strict logic which as indicated previously is not all illuminating, this is correct. But, behind the technical precision, there is an enveloping of insight to be derived from understanding a thinker's existential position or from his biography.

A thinker's historical situation, his language, his educational background, his religious, orientation or even his sexual biography can reveal as much about his philosophy as the narrow application of logic might do. The genetic fallacy is technically true, yet true only within the accepted logic of a specific age. Beyond that, what it states could itself be labeled a fallacy in a broad cultural sense. (75)

Shakespeare was a master in revealing the difference between a person's expressed ideas and the inner motivations governing them. (76) Consider the difference between the seemingly enlightened governance exercised by Claudius and his inner thoughts of murder and revenge. (77) Likewise, a philosopher's public and private lives should not be bifurcated. It is possible to interpret the ideas of Schopenhauer or Nietzsche in terms of strict logic, yet to do so would generate an enormous deception and eliminate a wide range of insight as to the genesis or meaning of their thought.

The Love of Wisdom-2

In light of the above, let us examine the love of wisdom as more of an emotion rather than a rational motivation. The one thing philosophers are supposed to do is to love wisdom. In the ancient Greek language, 'philos' means love and 'sophia' means wisdom. But, here again we confront problems with language.

In the ancient dialect, 'sophia' could also be translated as self-knowledge, instruction or absolute truth. In any case, as indicated previously, the love of wisdom is not specific to philosophy. Artists, poets, scientists, theologians and many others have also be known to love wisdom for its own sake.

In addition, during the 20th Century, some analytic philosophers have not been known to stress the development of wisdom, but rather of understanding as defined by a narrow language analysis. (78) If wisdom is defined as insight coming into action, the genesis of action has not been the goal of many analytic philosophers or even of post-modernists.

However, on a deeper level, what does the phrase 'love of wisdom' really mean? Is it similar to the love of mankind or that of a specific individual? In different contexts, the meaning of the term love can be quite disparate. In the context of persons, love is more bodily, visceral or emotional while the 'love of wisdom' is more of an intellectual value or desire.

There are funerals for persons, yet there has never been a funeral for an idea although some philosophical ideas truly deserve one. In a conflict between the two, it is evident that the 'love of persons' would be the stronger emotion or at least should be. On display here is the mixture of cognitive and emotional intelligence.

It should be noted that a philosopher must do more than simply love wisdom. He must act upon that love by developing specific knowledge within the field of philosophy and expanding upon it by creating his own philosophical ideas. This may involve the difficult task of questioning the value of truth itself or even contemplating the possibility that truth may be generated from false procedures or even a false science. Consider the development of the science of chemistry from the obviously flawed attempt to turn base metal into gold which indirectly generated a fair degree of knowledge about chemicals. (79) Also, consider how the social chaos of the French Revolution generated a continuous series ofa questioning about the nature of society which was a major factor in the development of the science of sociology. Falsehood may open a pathway to truth and chaos may lay its groundwork.

The Danger of Truth

The love of wisdom or truth may be dangerous as mankind rejects wisdom or truth in order to live a lie. That lie is the deliberate expulsion of truth for purposes of material gain or power. It takes an enormous amount of courage to dedicate your life to anything except what the great masses cherish and what they value is the mundane.

Thus, while the quest for wisdom or truth may bring great inner satisfaction, it may also place the philosopher at a massive disadvantage particularly in the economic realm. As Will Durant wrote, the poverty of Spinoza was due to the fact that he loved knowledge too much to be a successful man. (80) Success as defined, of course, in material terms.

A government despises no one more than a great philosopher. To be a great philosopher is to be the creator of new visions, alternative ideas and revolutionary values which may challenge the existing order of society. To be a great philosopher is equivalent to being a second government. No ruler desires a great philosopher such as a Plato or Kant, only lesser ones.

The Nature of Being

Being is embodied in man's individual finiteness. Existential being is singular, isolated, finite, biographical and is properly represented as 'my being' which is enriched by 'my world'. Thus, all delineations of being are isolated, mosaic delineations.

'My being' is existential. It is a deed-act derived from my existence. There is no such thing as being-in-itself or even human being as a broad abstraction. 'My being' is isolated, finite and engulfed within numerous bifurcations.

Men have biological, psychological and social similarities to others. Yet, there is something unique within every individual 'my being' which can be found in no one else: namely, a unique way of seeing the world, a unique vision of destiny or a novel capacity for transcendence. My biography is a unique record of a vision. Indeed, a philosophy in itself.

As Murray argued, all men are to some degree similar to all other men, to some other men and to no other man. (81) All men have a common biological structure while some men have similar social categories such as race, age, gender or ethnicity. Yet, in unique organic and social-psychological detail, each solitary individual is a singularity.

'My being' undergoes a unique socialization within a singular temporal epoch. 'My being' confronts a given in experience, a social 'a priori', of other minds and their folkways, mores or laws which are internalized as 'my world' in a manner unlike any other.

A's Heidegger wrote, we are 'thrown' into an already existing world of social facts. (82) It should be noted that there is no universal given in experience as 'my world' in exact detail is identical to no other. The question of inter-subjectivity is beyond our concern here, yet is achieved by second-order legitimations and congruencies based on language and other forms of symbolic accord. (83)

Prior to socialization, 'my being' knows no ethics, no law, no logic and is not dominated by anything as simple as a pleasure principle or for that matter any other rudimentary principle during the full course of its duration. Even Freud moved beyond the pleasure principle in his later writings. (84) Only the constraint of society through the use of formal and informal sanctions including although not isolated to the internalization of values or norms can control the direction of individual action. Hence, the necessity for the formation of society.

Those who have doubts or advocate anarchism should ponder the barbarism exhibited during the Black Death, the French Revolution or the American Civil War. The absence of society would give men total freedom, yet little security. Freedom is only a blessing under law.

What is called objectivity is largely a social phenomenon or a social game of pretense often described as the generalized other. (85) 'My being' knows no objectivity as here we go beyond the subjective to the core of nothingness.

There is a gap or void in being and we feel it in our moments of emptiness. Here we lust for the irrational, ponder the sadistic, hate what is good and savor murder, rape or incest. Glory amid the ruins! Pure destruction! Philosophy is a medium for the expression of what is unique within 'my being'.

In this sense, all philosophy is essentially autobiography and this includes the so-called objective mode of presentation which is merely an existential choice. Autobiography partially reveals 'my being' and is a map of 'my world', yet no more than a map as its full detail is never fully unfolded. 'My world' is not your world despite the congruencies of language and the functionality of institutional interdependence or social structure. A common world is as much a myth as the falsehood of pure being.

We all live in different worlds that are functionally related by social facts- language, culture, groups or social structure. (86) Unless revealed, 'my being' will not be included in the collective experience of mankind and shall be buried or hidden under a mound which you will never find. (87) Unlike science which deals with the more objective, a philosophical vision can never be duplicated.

If revealed, it is equivalent to the unfolding of a new world, a novel insight, a secular paradise or a new salvation. A total record of human wisdom is impossible, yet every novel idea enhances it. Even the insights of fools should be included. Philosophy is a humanity of humanity. Hence, essays, short stories, poetry, historical fiction, biographies and autobiographies are essential to philosophical expression in addition to non-fiction books or essays.

Every man is a story onto himself. He is a vision for good or for bad which illuminates the human condition. This illumination is singular and unrepeatable. McEwen described this individual uniqueness in the following manner. "Despite the irrational impulses of the human mind, each individual mind is a complex unity, l.e., all the complex sensations and desires of the present moment belong together in a unique way in the sense that 'my' experience is mine alone and cannot be possessed by anyone else." (88) Augustine's *Confessions* or the novels of Tolstoy would be excellent examples of this singularity. (89) Beauty of expression and insight are combined here. In autobiography, the profound may be revealed in the inconsequential, the eternal may be isolated in an instant, the universal may be seen in the particular and the unity of opposites may be plausible even to a mathematician. Autobiography is a lighthouse of illumination.

What is Truth?

What is truth? Truth does not lie in a proposition for all such excretions shall be disproven. Truth is embodied in 'my being' as 'my being' is my truth. This is what Jesus Christ meant when he said, "I am the truth". Truth is ontological and its ontology is 'my being'. It does not lie in the heavens and certainly not in propositions. The truth of propositions is transient whereas 'my being' is a deed-act of an eternal present. I have lived and my existence can never be duplicated. Christ again said, "I am the incarnation of all truth."

(As to the author's 'my being', enjoy the contradictions in this work and you will touch upon my truth as subsisting beyond what is relative since there is no relativity in ontology - only in propositions. But, more on that later.)

1. Simpson, William, K., (ed.), The Literature of Ancient Egypt, Yale University Press, New Haven, 1972.

2. Plato, The Republic, Benjamin Howett, trans., Heritage Illustrated Publishing, 2014.

3. Quine, W. V. O., Ontological Relativity and Other Essays, Columbia University Press, 1969.

4. Jung, Carl., Contributions to Analytical Psychology, (trans. H.G. & C. F. Baynes), Harcourt, Brace & Co., New York, 1928.

5. Campbell, Joseph., ed., The Portable Jung, Penguin Books, New York, 1976.

6. Chomsky, Norm, Aspects of the Theory of Syntax, M.I.T. Press, 1965.

7. Veblen, Thorsten, The Theory of the Leisure Class, Renaissance Classics, 2012.

8. Durkheim, Emile, The Rules of Sociological Method, W. O. Hills (trans.) The Free Press, 1982.

9. Whitehead, Alfred, N., Nature and Life, University of Chicago Press, 1934, Chapter 1.

10. Isaacson, Walter, Einstein: His life and Universe, Simon & Schuster, New York, 2007.

11. Otto, Rudolf, The Idea of the Holy, trans., J. W. Harvey, Basic Books, New York, 1970.

12. Shelly, Percy, Bysshe, Selected Poetry, Penguin Books, 1985, pg. 182.

13. Turner, J. W. M., Dido Building Carthage, National Gallery, London, 1815.

14. Schopenhauer, Arthur, Essays and Aphorisms, Penguin Books, 1970.

15. Delia, Edward, The Apocalypse, Vize Publications, 2004, pg. 2.

16. Plato, The Republic, Benjamin Howett, trans.. Heritage Illustrated Publishing, 2014.

17. Ibid.

18. Schopenhauer, Arthur, The World as Will and Representation, trans. E. F. J. Payne, Dover, 1966, Vol. I.

19. Popper, Karl, The Open Society and Its Enemies, Princeton University Press, 2013, pgs. 81-147.

20. Donald, David, Lincoln, Simon & Schuster, New York, 1995, pg. 176.

21. Stanley, Thomas, Pythagoras: His Life and Teaching, James Waserman, ed., Ibis Press, 2015.

22. Berkeley, George, Principles of Human Knowledge and the Dialogues, Roger, Woolhouse, ed., Penguin Books, New York, 2004.

23. Nietzsche, Frederick, Beyond Good and Evil, Millennium Publications, New York, 2014, pg. 3.

24. Machiavelli, Nicolo, The Prince, Dover Thrift Editions, New York, 1992, Pgs. 47-62.

25. Plato, The Republic, trans., Benjamin Howett, Heritage Illustrated Publishing, 2014.

26.Goffman, Erving, The Presentation of Self in Everyday Life, Anchor Books, N.Y., 1959.

27. Nietzsche, Frederick, Twilight of the idols, trans., Richard Rott, Hackett Publishing Co., 1996, pgs. 12-18.

28. Harl, Kenneth, W., The Peleponnesian War, The Teaching Co., Virginia, 2007, Vol. 1, pg. 266.

29. Goffman, Erving, The Presentation OF Self in Everyday Life, Anchor Books, New York, 1959.

30. Freud, Sigmund, An Outline of Psychoanalysis, 2nd Edition, trans. James Strachey, W.W. Norton and Co., NY, 1949.

31. Mannheim, Karl., Ideology and Utopia, trans., Louis Wirth & Edward Shils, Harcourt, Inc., New York, 1936, pgs. 55-59.

32. Guthrie, W.K.C., Socrates, Cambridge University Press, Cambridge, U.K., 1971, pgs. 105-110.

33. Brinkerhoff, D., Ortega, S., Weltz, R., Essentials of Sociology, 9" Edition, Wadsworth, NY, pg. 36.

34. Heidegger, Martin, Basic Writings, ed. David Krell, Harper Collins, New York, 2008, pg. 143-212.

35. Harman, G., Lepore, E., eds., A Companion to W. V. O. Quine, Wiley Blackwell, 2014, pgs. 236-263.

36. Burnet, John, Early Greek Philosophy, London & Edinburgh, Adam & Charles Black, 1892.

37. Delia, Edward, The Apocalypse, Vize Publications, New York, 2004, pgs. 2-3.

38. Whitehead, Alfred, N., Process and Reality, The Free Press, NY, 1978. pgs. 208-218.

39. Burnet, John, Early Greek Philosophy, London & Edinburgh, Adam & Charles Black, 1892.

40. Thorne, Kip, S., Black Holes and Time Warps: Einstein's Outrageous Legacy, W.W. Norton & Co., NY & London, 1994.

41. Kant, Immanuel, A Critique of Pure Reason, trans. J. M. D. Meiklejohn, Pacific Publishing Studio, 2011.

42. Goldstein, Rebecca, Incompleteness, W.W. Norton & Co., New York, pgs. 207-262.

43. Hartshorne, Robin, Geometry: Euclid and Beyond, Springer, New York, 2000, pgs. 7-51.

44.. Laugwitz, Detlef, Bernhard Riemann, Turning Points in the Conception of Mathematics, trans. Abe Shenitzer, Springer Science & Business Media, New York, 1996, pgs. 272-277.

45. Popper, Karl, The Poverty of Historicism, Routledge, London & NY, 1999.

46. Lyotard, Jean-Francols, The Postmodern Condition: A Report on Knowledge, trans., Goeff Bennington & Brian Massoml, University of Minnesota Press, Minneapolis, MN, 1989, pgs. 27-41.

47. McEwen, William, P., The Problem of Social Scientific Knowledge, Bedminester Press, New Jersey, 1963.

48. Harl, Kenneth, The Peleponnesian War, The Teaching Co., Virginia, 2007, Vol. 1, pg. 175.

49. Merton, Robert, K., Social Theory and Social Structure, The Free Press, New York, 1968, PGS. 48-53,

50. Feyerabend, Paul, Against Method: Outline of an Anarchistic Theory of Knowledge, 4th Edition, Verso Books, New York, 2010.

51. Hume, David, An Enquiry Concerning Human Understanding, 2nd Edition, ed., Eric Steinberg, Hackett Publishing Co., Cambridge, 1993.

52. Shelly, Percy, Bysshe, Poetical Works, ed., Thomas Hitchins, London University Press, London, 1960, pg. 523.

53. Campbell, Joseph, ed., The Portable Jung, Penguin Books, New York, 1976.

54. Feyerabend, Paul, Against Method: Outline of an Anarchistic Theory of knowledge, 10™ Edition, Velsa Books, New York, 2010.

55. Campbell, Joseph, ed., The Portable Jung, Penguin Books, New York, 1976.

56. Hume, David., An Enquiry Concerning Human Understanding, trans. By L.. Beauchamp, Oxford University Press, Oxford & NY, 1999, pgs. 134-147.

57. Ayer, A.J., Language, Truth and Logic, Dover Publications Inc., NY, 1952, pgs. 49-51.

58. Aristotle, The Organon, edited by Roger Bishop Jones, NY, 2016, pgs. 59-111.

59. Delia, Edward, The Apocalypse, Vize Publications, NY, 2004, pgs. 2-4.

60. Freud, Sigmund, The Interpretation of Dreams, trans. & ed. by James Strachey, Basic Books, NY, 2010.

61. Jung, Carl, G., The Collective Works of C.G. Jung- Archetypes and Collective Unconscious, trans. & ed. by Gerhard Adler & F.C. Hull, Princeton University Press, NJ, 1980, pgs. 42-53.

62. ibid.

63. Taylor, Richard, Metaphysics, Foundation of Philosophy Series, Englewood Cliffs, Prentice-Hall, NJ, 1963.

64. Kaufman, Walter, ed. Existentialism from Dostoevsky to Sartre, Penguin Group, NY, 1975, pgs. 280-374.

65, Freud, Sigmund, The Interpretation of Dreams, trans. & ed. by James Strachey, Basic Books, NY, 2010.

66. Ibid.

67. Strathern, Paul, Mendeleyev's Dream; The Quest for the Elements, St. Martin's Press, NY, 2001.

68. Hass, Laurene, Merleau-Ponty's Philosophy, Indiana State University Press, IN, 2008, pgs. 74-99.

69. Kant, Immanuel, Critique of Pure Reason, ed. Marcus Weigett, Penguin Classics, NY, 2007.

70. Jaspers, Karl, Anselm and Nicholas of Cusa, ed. by Hannah Arendt, trans. by Ralph Mannheim, Harcourt, Brace & Jovanovach, NY & London, 1966, pgs. 4-25.

71. Berger Peter, & Luckmann, Thomas, The Social Construction of Reality: A Treatise on the Sociology of Knowledge, Anchor Books, NY, 1966, pg. 183.

72. Spinoza, Benedict, Ethics, trans. Edwin Corley, Penguin Books, NY, 1996.

73. Branden, Nathaniel, The Psychology of Self Esteem, Jessey-Bass, San Francisco. 2001.

74. Gerth, Hans, & Mills, C.W., From Max Weber: Essays in Sociology, Oxford University Press, NY, 1946.

75. Foucault, Michel, Madness and Civilization, trans. by Richard Howard, Vintage Books, NY, 1988, pg. 281.

76. Hazlitt, William, Characters in Shakespeare's Plays, Moden Perlance, NY, 2013.

77. tbid, pgs. 77-84.

78. Ayer, A. J., Language, Truth and Logic, Dover Publications, NY, 1952.

79. Bartlett, Robert, Real Alchemy, IBIS Press, FL, 2000.

80. Durant, Will, The Story of Philosophy, Simon & Schuster, NY, 1961, pgs. 146-196.

81. Murray, Henry, & Kluckhohm, Clyde, Personality in Nature, Society and Culture, Knoph, NY, 1953.

82. Steiner, George, Martin Heidegger, University of Chicago Press, IL, 1987, pgs. 73-126.

83. Berger, Peter & Luckmann, Thomas, The Social Construction of Reality: A Treatise on the Sociology of Knowledge, Anchor Books, NY, 1966.

84. Freud, Sigmund, Beyond the Pleasure Principle, ed. by James Strachey, Liveright Publishing Co., NY, 1989, pgs. 1-28.

85. Mead, George, Herbert, Mind, Self and Society, University of Chicago Press, IL, 2015, pgs. 152-163.

86. Brinkerhoff, David, & Weitz, Rose & Ortega, Susanne, Essentials of Sociology, Wadsworth, CA, 9th Edition, pgs. 29-92.

87. Masters, Edgar, Lee, Spoon River Anthology, Dover, NY, 1992, pg. 53.

88. McEwen, Willian, Enduring Satisfaction, The Philosophical Library, NY, 1949, pg. 123.

89. Augustine, Saint, Saint Augustine's Confessions, trans. by Henry Chadwick, Oxford University Press, NY, 1991.

Chapter 3

Alternative Conceptions of Philosophy

Although there is no limit to the number of intelligent suggestions as to what philosophy is, no interpretation has been universally accepted. The reason is that these suggestions are never clear in regard to identifying exactly what method a philosopher should utilize which is acceptable to all others in its entirety. Some thinkers such as Descartes and Husserl have had great influence in this direction, yet neither has achieved universal recognition. As stated earlier, the impossibility of establishing universal definitions seems to doom this possibility.

To Plato, a philosopher should meditate upon the essences of ideal forms. (1) To Anselm, a thinker must, through faith and reflection, contemplate the nature of a being greater than which anything can be conceived. (2) To Hume, a skeptical philosophy must still provide an intelligent commentary on human nature. (3) To Kant, a philosopher must construct 'a priori' knowledge. (4) To Schopenhauer's mind, intelligent reflection must focus in on the blind, irrational Will in nature. (5) To Nietzsche, a creative genius must, above all, be a creator of values. (6) To Ayer, the focus of a philosopher should be the analysis of language. (7) To C. I. Lewis, a philosopher should study the pragmatic 'a priori'. (8) To Whitehead, a philosopher should provide a categorical scheme through which every element of our experience may be interpreted. (9) To Husserl, a philosopher should investigate phenomena. (10) To Heidegger, a philosophy should be concerned with the original study of being. (11)

We may continue this list of definitions to infinity, yet each of them would exclude as much as it includes. There is no universally accepted definition of philosophy and there will never be. All definitions have the same nemesis: namely, alternative definitions. This statement is not a relativism and does not imply that every definition is of equal value. Indeed, the opposite is maintained here. Obviously, a definition is being offered.

(As an existential affirmation, I am possessed of no false ambition that this book will provide the final answer to the difficult question as to the meaning of philosophy. My only desire is that it will clarify certain issues which will stimulate further research on this topic. The meaning of philosophy remains as the primary problem of philosophy from which all other significant problems stem.)

There are several reasons for the disparity of philosophical definitions. First, philosophy has no definite subject matter or realm of inquiry. While there are disagreements about the meaning of several other disciplines, a more general consensus can be discerned in the conventional wisdom there. Many sociologists would agree that sociology is the study of society and most psychologists would agree that psychology is the study of behavior. Most biologists would concur that biology is the science of life or living matter.

There may be disagreements as to what society, behavior or living matter consists of, yet there is a basic focus there. This is lacking in philosophy. Philosophers can be concerned with anything from mechanics to theology or from questions concerning God to queries about whether machines can think. The field is too broad in its range of concerns. Some argue that this is the strength of philosophy: namely, that a philosopher must be a master of the universe of discourse. On the other hand, it also renders impossible any attempt to establish an acceptable definition.

Another reason for the lack of a universal definition is that philosophy is as much a product of instinct or emotion as it is of rational deliberation. Philosophy is a product of singular men and women with a definite psychology or character as shaped by a unique social environment. It is as much a sum of bone or flesh as it is of logic. While this is also true of other disciplines, it is much more so of philosophy given the lack of subject focus as discussed above.

A third reason for the lack of consensus is the omnipresence of change. Change affects all academic disciplines, but in philosophy a change anywhere in the universe of discourse can bring enormous modifications in philosophical theories. A theologian may be unconcerned with changes in computer technology and does not have to modify his ideas as a consequence of those changes, yet a philosopher has to be concerned since those modifications may generate novel ideational queries of profound consequence in his discipline. Philosophy can be affected by changes in the fields of art, music, law, social science, natural science, theology, mechanics, medicine, government, dance, theater and many other fields. As new disciplines are invented, a philosophy of that discipline usually arises.

Yet, despite this diversity among definitions and for purposes of academic integrity, it is necessary to examine in more detail a few of these alternative definitions.

The Popper Thesis

Karl Popper believed that philosophy represented and embodied a reaction to the transition from a traditional to a more advanced civilization which mandated a drastic change in mentality. (12) That mentality was primarily philosophical in nature. In traditional societies, no distinction was made between natural and conventional law.

The natural and the social realm were thought to be fixed and identical. Whether living or non-living, natural objects (trees, animals or rocks) were thought to have the same ontological status as social facts (beliefs, rituals or groups). Both were fixed and unchanging.

In more advanced societies, it was evident that social facts were not fixed, but could be changed by human intervention. The transition gave rise to questions concerning the status of social conventions and psychologically to the shock of living in an unstable world where beliefs or ideas are in flux. This change led to anxiety and the ensuing questioning served as a stimulus to philosophy.

In analyzing this perspective, it must be said that massive social change is often a catalyst to philosophical inquiry. Heraclitus, as noted previously, was among the first to recognize the flux in the universe. One of his famous fragments stated that the universe was a scrap heap scattered at random - a fragment that the present author has great sympathy toward. There is little doubt that the transition from the primitive to a more advanced life style gave rise to value questions which must be recognized as philosophical.

Yet, we should not go too far with this theory. As in all theories, it does not explain all the facts in its domain. There are two great limitations here. First, it is probable that philosophical concerns did exist in primitive societies.

All societies have deviants who question conventional ideas. Also, there are always singular individuals who undergo abnormal states of mind or divergent degrees of cognitive awareness. This condition often results in anomie which in turn often gives rise to metaphysical queries. Moreover, it is doubtful that any society is so primitive as to be devoid of secondary socialization. (13) Secondary socialization takes ús beyond the taken-for-granted 'home world' of primary socialization in early childhood. The stimulus for philosophy would then exist in the primitive world.

Second, the term primitive here is used by Popper in a simple, unsophisticated manner. He seems to be referring to the world of Ancient Greece before Thales. Yet, there were many other primitive societies at that time all over the earth which were in fact quite different as there are many primitive cultures in the world at the present time. Popper's analysis is, therefore, based on one singular era and his conclusions cannot be applied to all other primitive cultures. It goes without saying that his research is not backed by any detailed anthropological analysis.

In the end, Popper does not tell us what philosophy is, but only that it consists of questioning a taken-for-granted reality after the transition from primitive to modern consciousness. Yet, questioning is important in all disciplines. It is not only questioning, but awareness of 'my being' which is the key to philosophy. All people have a biography and their experience in this 'life-world' gives rise to odd musings. They may not be metaphysical ones at first, yet these musings may pave a path there through a combination of emotional awareness and intelligent reflection. Of course, the status of philosopher must then emerge in the social structure of any society and with that status comes a symbolic universe to support it. Whether primitive or modern, all people have a biography which is the key to philosophy.

One further word is necessary. It is true that advanced civilization and a surplus are necessary for the emergence of philosophy. What is said above is simply that there was some pre-philosophical thought in the primitive world. A reversion to that world would diminish philosophy as happened after the fall of the Western Roman Empire which is today called a 'Dark Age' perhaps with some correctness.

Philosophy as a Way of Life

Epictetus proposed a completely different meaning to philosophy. (14) Philosophy, he argued, is a discipline which should provide a way of living. Cognitive understanding is one thing, yet wisdom is another. Wisdom is insight coming into action. Wisdom utilizes knowledge as a guide to living with quality. The quality could be happiness, success or self-realization.

Spinoza clearly exhibited this. sort of wisdom in life. (15) He actually lived in a manner consistent with his philosophy. Yet, in the 21th Century, this is rarely done. Analytic philosophers or even post-modernists seem to believe that this conception is naïve or even absurd. They are concerned with the analysis of language or science or epistemological queries which have little to do with day to day living. This may enhance knowledge or the understanding, yet rarely does it have anything to do with everyday life.

This conception was prevalent in Ancient Roman times with the advent of stoicism or in the writings of the cynics. (16) There is a kernel of truth in their ideas, yet none has been universally accepted. The reason is that life is too complex for any solitary, singular individual to provide a general guide for living based on philosophical maxims or formulas. There are thousands of cultures and even a greater number of subcultures or countercultures in the world which means thousands upon thousands of interpretations of the meaning of life for any universal formula to cover all of them with one massive insight.

We must recall the famous dictum that no universal is worth a damn. While this may be an exaggeration, life is in large part concerned with the specific, the concrete or the particular. This is the key to the meaning of meaning.

This attempted definition excludes too much. Philosophers must be concerned with a wide range of issues besides problems connected with their personal existence. Yet, they should also use their minds to provide a way of living better- that is, in terms of their own lives. To go beyond that is arrogance and at times we all display that type of arrogance. Only by examining 'my being' in its personal and social vectors can the meaning of my solitary existence be found. The meaning of my life and my death by anticipation may be located only by introspection.

Socrates, as interpreted by Plato, said the unexamined life is not worth living. This is true, yet what must be examined is 'my being'- which is not your being or Socrates' being- in its full autobiographical detail. This examination, by the way, does not necessarily have to be a philosophical one.

I would recommend that as a scholar, but a person's life may have meaning without philosophy. If you are concerned with more mundane matters, that would be the key to your being. Meaning and truth need not be universal.

Philosophy as an Evaluation of Society

A related conception is that philosophy should establish theories which either justify or condemn social institutions or their goals. In this conception, philosophers do not create values or norms, but attempt to facilitate or retard their realization. In other words, thinkers are not so much proposing an entire manner of living, but rather evaluating those which already exist.

They may do this either by writing books justifying the divine right of kings or by producing philosophical manuscripts condemning institutions such as capitalism. (17) At times, utopias may be proposed to demonstrate the ideal form of society. (18) Some of these have been taken seriously, others less so.

This conception begins on firmer grounds than the previous, yet does have one great defect: namely, it renders philosophy to be little more than an ideology or utopia. (19) As an ideology, philosophy would serve the interests of conservative governments by legitimating existing institutions and thereby could be regarded as a puppet of those interests. Edmund Burke's writing on the French Revolution would be a good example. (20) As a utopia, philosophers would serve to facilitate revolutionary activity and be of service to extreme radicals. The writings of Marx would clearly be a good example here. (21) In either case, philosophy would be rendered as an idle servant of selfish or partisan interests rather than an objective pursuit of truth. Objectivity demands that such bias should be held to a minimum. At least, the conception of objectivity as held by contemporary philosophers of science.

This conception is neither sound nor does it provide a good definition of philosophy. Philosophy is concerned with many things besides an analysis of the nature of society such as art, music, theology, epistemology and general metaphysics. It excludes too múch and does not identify the key to the meaning of meaning. That key is 'my being' and any analysis of societal relations must begin there, end there or posit nothing at all. The starting point is in myself. Pure being is nothing.

If we do wish to construct an analysis of society, philosophers should do so only after an intensive study of the social sciences with an emphasis on sociology and political science. The best writings on the nature of society can be found in the work of Talcott Parsons and Robert Merton among others. (22)

This is not an endorsement of functionalism, but rather an appeal to social philosophers to consult the extensive research in social science before rendering premature conclusions. Times are different than in the past long before the development of the social sciences. Plato, Aristotle, Hobbes, Spinoza and others wrote powerful commentary on political philosophy, yet social science was in its infancy then. Change is continuous and a reassessment is necessary.

(As an existential affirmation, it should be noted that this appeal does not contradict the previous notion that no scientific statement is certain and is at best a high probability proposition. We must use the tools we have even though they may be relegated to dust in the infinite myriads of space and time.)

The Kantian Thesis

Kant believes that the key to philosophy is the establishment of the 'a priori', not only in, theoretical, but also in practical reason. (23) Knowledge to him is a constructed product- constructed by the 'a priori categories in the human mind. What we know is phenomena and beyond them are the noumena of which we may never know.

The establishment and understanding of these categories is the task of philosophy. Quality, quantity, relation, and modality are 'a priori' modes of interpretation by which the mind organizes the raw material lying ready to the senses. Space and time are not realities in themselves, but rather 'a priori' forms without which there can be no intelligible notion of causation.

Other thinkers have built upon Kant's foundation. This is especially true of Schopenhauer who renders the noumena to be the Absolute Will in nature and of C.I. Lewis who advocated the notion of the pragmatic 'a priori'. (24)

This conception of the discipline is powerful and the world is a constructed product in the sense that we know nothing more than phenomena. All else is simply pure conjecture. There are, however, a few basic problems with this definition. First, in the tradition of Schopenhauer, we cannot accept the idea of practical reason.

All philosophy is theoretical and remains so no matter what efforts are made to render it practical. It is possible for a solitary individual to apply certain maxims or philosophical notions which were developed theoretically to his personal life or to the wider community, yet there is no necessity in this application. Only folkways and mores which are learned through socialization may impose an external constraint upon behavior. (25) These folkways and mores are not always rational, but are often quite irrational or arbitrary as developed over centuries of experience.

Second, Kant's table of categories is too individualistic and does not account for the social development of these modes of thought. Quantity, quality, relation or modality may be conceived quite differently in diverse cultures of civilizations. (26) Third, as McEwen noted, these categories or 'a priori' projections of the mind must themselves have subsisted prior to their entry into human mentality in order to account for both their presence and pervasive influence. (27)

Finally, even if these flaws were circumvented, a sound world-view must transcend any mere consideration of categories. Philosophy also deals with the irrational and what is both beyond and below human attention. Man is more than a stream of categories, but a presence, a deed-act, a biographical singularity and a component in the fabric of total comprehension. The subjectivity of man cannot be negated by any attempted reduction to objective considerations. 'My being' is beyond. It may be reached for, yet never touched.

Philosophy as an Activity

Many thinkers consider philosophy to be an activity, not a term to be defined. (28) Questioning, counterargument or continual debate is seen as the key to refine issues and generate clarity. Unlike poetry or literary genre, philosophy must meet the test of critical discussion, contradictory evidence and rebuttal. No doubt, to some degree it does..

Yet, we must not go too far with this idea. It is also possible to debate about poetry, novels, short stories, plays, music or art. Consider the critical discussion concerning Shakespeare's tragedies. Moreover, this idea of continual debate shares the limitation described previously: namely, debate obviously utilizes language.

Within the structure of language, universal definitions are not attainable. Thinkers can comprehend no more in insight than the categorical apparatus in any vernacular allows. Thus, the continual necessity to invent new words in the vain attempt to leap toward the huge complex of ideas or feelings to which the existing language points, yet does not embrace. To refer to the discipline as an activity does not circumvent this limitation.

It simply denies a final resting point to the process which is not much different from the ideas advocated earlier. Our attempt to define philosophy has no false ambition such as to provide the ultimate meaning of the term. When others conceive philosophy as an activity, they confuse the activity observed in the process of thinking or in intense debate with the significance or meaning of the quest.

The point is not merely to engage in an activity, but rather to answer the most perplexing queries of mankind. Activities always have a fascination and all human endeavors can be described as an activity.

Some, however, are more meaningful than others and philosophy is one of these.

Philosophy as a Science

There are many thinkers who believe that philosophy should restructure itself to be more of a science. (29) The most brazen attempt to redirect philosophy in this direction may be found in the writings of the logical positivist, A.J. Ayer. (30)

He argued that a philosopher should concentrate on the analysis of the meaning of language which he contends has meaning only in terms of the verification hypothesis: namely, the meaning of a proposition is its method of verification. Verification in turn depends upon sense data which either affirm or nullify the truth of the proposition in actuality or in principle. Otherwise, propositions are not only false, but meaningless. Exit metaphysics, at least in the mind of this ideational explorer.

In evaluating this approach, let us keep in mind that A.J. Ayer was a young man when he advocated this. Being young, he displayed all the enthusiasm of a neophyte. No doubt, this verification hypothesis is one of the most simplistic, absurd proposals in the entire history of philosophy. There are several reasons for this. First, scientific propositions are not verified merely by sense-data, but by operational or control procedures and by an analysis of the factors of internal or external validity. Second, Ayer failed to realize that language contains universals which are metaphysical in nature and unverifiable. (31) Third, Ayer uses the so-called laws of logic in his analysis which, as discussed earlier, are incapable of proof. Finally, the inner nature of our mentality as expressed in value judgements cannot be verified in this manner, yet they embody an essential inventory of insight regarding the human condition.

B.F. Skinner, in similar manner, attempted to enhance the potency of psychology as a science by arbitrarily eliminating internal mental structures and then reducing that science to the study of overt, observable behavior. (32) Yet, this would eliminate from scientific scrutiny significant value judgements, notions of god or immortality and interpretations of life that are needed in any proper study of mankind.

The great questions of human existence transcend any such puny analysis. Man's existence cannot be reduced to an abstract formula. It is concrete, singular and mysterious. No simple verification or behaviorist formula can negate that basic truth. Moreover, this view fails to understand that philosophy depends upon choice and a thinker may reject the dictates of a vast, impersonal reason. 'My being' or my deed-act-transcends reason. It may accept or reject. If rejected, this has equal value to the choice of an objectivity.

This is ultimately the one limitation in Aristotle's or Whitehead's quest for descriptive categories. 'My being' may be broken down into categories by scientifically orientated philosophers or incurable metaphysicians, yet my inner self, as an existential act, is non-scientific and non-categorical. It is a non-objectified deed-act.

The Phenomenologist Thesis

The three great phenomenologists are Husserl, Heidegger and Merleau-Ponty. (33) Husserl believed that philosophy must pursue the phenomenological method, Heidegger thought that this method opened the door to the original study of being and Merleau-Pointy believed that phenomenology must relate to the primal origin of the body.

All three of these thinkers have identified deep structures of meaning relating to the true essence of philosophy. We know nothing except phenomena and must infer all else by inference. In the process of inference comes philosophical wisdom, yet this wisdom finds its locus in the body.

There is, however, a process of subtraction here. First, the phenomenological method may not be exactly as Husserl describes it. Our interpretation of phenomena is directed, either by experience or genetic inheritance, to seek the origin of circumstances. Yet, this is simply an epistemological presupposition or a cognitive posit which may be directed in many diverse ways either by causation or functional integration or synchronicity. Phenomena may not have an essence and might be, in specific cases, a brute singularity with no essence whatsoever. This is Plato's great error in his assertion that philosophers should search for ideal forms or essences. He assumes that we can discern essences in every instance and does not envision that they might be nothing more than existential trivia.

Plurality, not unity is the great word of philosophy since plurality is constantly observed in phenomena. Fire is all. The singular, the partial or the unique will pave the way for understanding phenomena and with this a comprehension of the human condition.

Second, as Merleau-Ponty insisted, the locus of interpretation must be in the body, Phenomena as perceived by the eye and the other senses is a presentation in the body and would be perceived differently by other organisms. "The world is my representation" speaks the truth. (34) All else is inference. Yet, phenomena are not unified and in no manner can my perception of phenomena be known to be the same as yours. 'My world' (i.e. phenomena) is not the same as your world. (35) Nor is my body the same as your body. There is no generalized or common body, but only individual bodies which are quite singular and often with different apperceptions. My world, my body - this must be the focus of the phenomenologist. A common world, assuming it exists, is the great achievement of language, culture and social structure.

Third, Heidegger is correct that phenomenology must open the door to the original study of being as in the case of the ancient Greeks. Being as a common term, however, must be rejected. Being-in-itself is nothing. It is a misapprehension. It is singular being or my being which is the key. 'My being' meaning every person's singular existence. Philosophy envelops the unfolding of the collective 'my being' of every unique individual, yet nonetheless fails in the endeavor to embody the total sum of 'my being': that is, the 'my being' of all existing individuals.

The unfolding of 'my being' is a choice and in many cases that choice is to say no. This is why the history of philosophy must to some degree be a 'fake'. It excludes the wisest individuals who must have existed in every advanced civilization who had transcended the vanity to be known for their wisdom. (36) Some of the wisest individuals that the present author has ever known would not be included in the history of philosophy, yet their wisdom still shines in a benighted would.

The Rise of the Meta

Another idea of what philosophy constitutes is that it discerns the 'meta' of all disciplines or thoughts. In fact, during the 20th Century, one could find what may be described as the triumph of the 'meta'. Metaphysics was discerned to be meaningless by the logical positivists. (37)

It was concluded that thinkers should not render metaphysical statements, but rather analyze them. In short, to engage in meta-metaphysics. This philosophical cancer cell led to others. One should not engage in ethics, but rather meta-ethics: namely, they

71

should not render ethical precepts or state what is good or evil, but rather analyze those conceptions. Aesthetics must also exist to be replaced by meta-aesthetics and so on.

In examining all this, let us first say that few philosophers are as superficial as Ayer or the other logical positivists. Contrary to popular opinion, George Edward Moore, was not a meta-ethical philosopher despite his conception of the naturalistic fallacy. (38) He was interested in stating which things are good or evil and how we ought to act. (39) The great questions of human existence should not be eschewed and replaced by a narrow-minded analysis of terminology. Meta-metaphysics and other approaches of this nature can reveal much insight, but should not replace the original disciplines of philosophy. We need both metaphysics and meta-metaphysics.

The arrangement of traditionalism combined with a 'meta' is the desirable one. The problem with this conception is that it doesn't state what should be examined. That is 'my being'. A phenomenological analysis of the dynamics of 'my being' is the key to both traditional and 'meta' philosophy: namely, the former examining the exploration of 'my being' while the latter analyzing the language employed in the exploration. This will produce a 'map' of my unique self, yet not its complete ontology. That is the void or hole in all phenomenological entailment. The method is clearly primarily autobiographical and secondarily biographical. The former is the 'map' of 'my being' provided by introspection, the latter presents the impressions of others as it relates to that unique self in society. Both involve role playing since internally and externally we all wear masks. The quest is to get behind the masks as much as possible.

The Defects of Categorical Analysis

This is the reason that the categorical approach to philosophy as provided in Whitehead or earlier in Aristotle is defective. One can never develop a complete, coherent or comprehensive categorical scheme by which every element of our experience can be interpreted. (40) 'Our experience' - this is no more than a metaphor. The important phrase is 'my experience' since my experience can never be the same as yours. Similar, perhaps, but no more than that.

This is the achievement of intersubjectivity. Generic categories do not necessarily relate to me. The categories of Whitehead, as those of Kant or Aristotle before him, are mostly a product of Western Civilization and cannot pertain to all peoples across the globe to say nothing of eccentric individuals. 'My being' may reject these categories and devour any notion of 'our common world'.

Erving Goffman made this clear in his presentation of symbolic interactionism. (41) He stressed that in order to comprehend other people one must consider how they are interpreting the world. This can be easily seen in the case of children or the mentally ill. A child does not view the world in a manner similar to an adult. A child psychologist tries to reconstruct the child's interpretation. The same is true of the mentally ill. Generic categories are of little help here. The mentally ill do not think in terms of generic categories.

This is wooden iron. The dull fact is that everyone must be approached individually and not in terms of the general. Each person has a unique personal history or experience which is not equal to any other's life world. To know where someone's going you must understand where they have been at least in terms of one's internal consciousness.

These considerations also negate Whitehead's conception of a pluralistic, interconnected universe. (42) There is no 'a priori' reason why the universe must be interconnected or subsist as a unity. This is an epistemological assumption or an arbitrary posit by a mentality directed toward the origin of circumstances. The basic principles behind enquiry were established by the empiricist philosophers of the 18th century. (43) Yet, epistemological rules do not and cannot relate to the basic ontology of the universe. Association in space and time or causation are particularly useful in this realm of the cosmos, yet it cannot be assumed that they apply beyond that symbolic universe.

(As an existential affirmation, it seems to this singular author that the urge for unity is tied to the rise of the scientific conception of philosophy. True, it was assumed as a postulate in the thinking of the ancient Greeks, yet it was thinkers such as Spencer or Comte that extended this assumption to its logical extreme. To the latter, disunity or chaos were incompatible with science.

Hence, the need for the assumption that reality is an ordered unity. Yet, what we observe are phenomena of all types and we cannot know their origin except by an arbitrary epistemological posit. In the end, all of science should be reduced to phenomenology since we do not know of an external world apart from an applied bodily interpretation. Phenomenological science is not an absurdity. It is science apart from the former which is the nemesis.)

Autobiography is the Key

What may be discerned from this? The phenomenological method must be autobiographical and the key is introspection. Only by looking within ourselves can be even begin to examine phenomena. That is, as long as we comprehend the wide gap between our mentality and all else. Epistemology must never again determine ontology. The mission of philosophy is to find the truth or the divine within our own being.

Now, this idea can be traced back to Plato and more recently to the 19th Century New England Transcendentalists. (45) Yet, the latter's views if extended could lead to the 'fallacy of the universal man': namely, that all men and women too have a common nature or act upon the basis of the same principles. This assumption is denied here. There are thousands of divergent cultures which is equivalent to myriads upon myriads of interpretations of existence.

The phenomenological examination of 'my being' posits every individual as a unique entity with qualities or ideas found in no other person. A bland universalism is rejected. 'I am the truth!' This identification of truth and being is the key toward a reemergence of ancient Greek thought.

1. Plato, Six Great Dialogues, trans. Benjamin Jowett, Dover, Minneola, NY, 2007.

2. Anselm, Basic Writings, ed. & trans. by Thomas Williams, Hackett publishing, IN, 2007, pgs. 75-99.

3. Hume, David, A Treatise of Human Nature, ed. by David Fate Norton & Mary J. Norton, Oxford, NY, 2001.

4. Kant, Immanuel, Critique of Pure Reason, trans. By Marcus Weigelt & Max Muller, Penguin, NY, 2007.

5. Schopenhauer, Arthur, Essays and Aphorisms, trans. by R. J. Hollingdale, Penguin, NY, 2004, pgs. 66-77,

6. Nietzsche, Fredrick, On the Genealogy of Morals and Ecce Homo, ed. by Walter Kaufmann, Vintage, NY, 1989.

7. Ayer, A. J., Language, Truth and Logic, Dover, NY, 1952.

8. Lewis, C. I., Mind and the World Order: Outline of a Theory of Knowledge, Dover, NY, 1956.

9. Whitehead, Alfred, North., Process and Reality, ed. by David Ray Griffin & Donald W. Sherburne, Free Press, NY, 1978, pgs. 3-4.

10. Husserl, Edmund, Ideas: A General Introduction to Pure Phenomenology, trans. R. Boyce Gibson, Routledge, London & NY, 2012.

11. Heidegger, Martin., Being and Time, trans. by Martin Macquarrie & Edward Robinson, Harper & Row, 2008, pgs. 21-32.

12. Popper, Karl., The Oben Society and its Enemies, Princeton University Press, NJ, 2013, pgs. 33-81.

13. Berger, Peter, Luckmann, Thomas., The Social Construction of Reality: A Treatise on the Sociology of Knowledge, Anchor Books, NY 1966.

14. Epictetus, Enchiridion, ed. by Thomas Crawford, Dover, NY, 2004.

15. Nadler, Steven, Spinoza: A Life, Cambridge, University Press, Cambridge & NY, 1999.

16. Aurelius, Marcus, Meditations, trans. Walter Kaufman, Dover, 1997.

17. Marx, Karl, Capital: Volume 1, Penguin Books, NY, 1990.

18. More, Thomas, Utopia, Penguin, Books, NY, 2003.

19. Mannheim, Karl, Ideology and. Utopia: An Introduction to the Sociology of Knowledge, trans. By Louls Wirth & Edward Shills, Harcourt, Inc. NY, 1936, pgs: 59 to 169.

20. Burke, Edmund, Reflections on the. Revolution in France, Oxford, ed. by L. G. Mitchell, NY, 2009.

21. Marx, Karl, Capital: Volume 1, Penguin Books, NY, 1990.

22. Merton, Robert, K., Social Theory and Social Structure, The Free Press, 1968, NY.

23. Kant, Immanuel, Critique of Pure Reason, Feather Trail Press, NY, 2009.

24. Lewis, C. I., Mind and the World Order: Outline of a Theory of Knowledge, Dover Reprint, 1956.

25. Durkheim, Emile, The Rules of Sociological Method, The Free Press, NY, 2013, PGS. 20-29.

26. Kant, Immanuel, Critique of Pure Reason, Feather Trail Press, NY, 2009.

27. McEwen, William, Enduring Satisfaction, Philosophical Library, NY, 1949.

28. Wittgenstein, Ludwig, Philosophical Investigations, trans. by G.E.M. Anscombe, ed. by P.M.S. Hacker & Joachim Schulte, Wiley-Blackwell, MA, 2009.

29. Reichenbach, Hans, The Rise of Scientific Philosophy, University of California Press, CA, 1951, pgs. 303-326.

30. Ayer, A.J., Language, Truth and Logic, Dover, NY, 1952.

31. McEwen, Willlam, Enduring Satisfaction, Philosophical Library, NY, 1949.

32. Skinner, B.F., Beyond Freedom and Dignity, Hackett Publishing, IN, 2002.

33. Sokolowski, Robert, Introduction to Phenomenology, Cambridge University Press, NY, 2007.

34. Schopenhauer, Arthur, The World as Will and Representation, Vol. 1, trans. By E.F.J. Payne, Dover, NY, 1969, pg. 3.

35. Della, Edward, The Apocalypse, Vize, NY, 2004, pgs. 2-3.

36. Moyer, Bill, A World of Ideas, Doubleday, NY, 1989.

37. Ayer, A.J., Language, Truth and Logic, Dover, NY, 1952.

38. Moore, G.E., Principia Ethica, Dover, NY, 2004, pgs. 12-20.

39. Ibid, pgs. 205-221.

40. Whitehead, Alfred, North, Process and Reality, ed. by David Ray Griffin & Donald W. Sherburne, The Free Press, NY, 1978.

41. Goffman, Erving, The Presentation of Self in Everyday Life, Anchor Books, NY, 1959.

42. Lowe, Victor, Understanding Whitehead, John Hopkins University press, MD, 1966.

43. Woolhouse, R.S., The Empiricists, Oxford, NY, 1988.

44. Thompson, John, A., Herbert Spencer, Forgotten Books, NY, 2016.

45. Emerson, Ralph, W., The Essential Writings of Ralph Waldo Emerson, Random House, NY, 2000.

Chapter 4
Of What Use Is Philosophy?

Unthinking mortals and a few thinking ones too believe that philosophy has no use or little use. To them, it is simply a form of intellectual conspicuous consumption or at best a meaningless game. To the contrary, few things are more important than a nation's philosophical tradition. If history is destiny, then the history of philosophy is its main component. Let us examine the uses of philosophy.

Philosophers Create Symbols

First, philosophers delineate symbols which determine the destiny of a nation. Sages during the Age of Enlightenment clearly affected the ideals of the French Revolution and the all-important Declaration of the Rights of Man and Citizen. (1) Those ideals have never perished and have inspired revolutionary activity form the 19th to the 20th Centuries. Likewise, the ideas of John Locke influenced Thomas Jefferson's ideals as expressed in the Declaration of Independence. (2) Augustine's philosophy definitely influenced the theology of Martin Luther and the development of the Protestant Ethic. (3) On the negative side, 19th Century German philosophy helped determine the mind of Adolf Hitler and the horror of the Third Reich. (4)

The most bereft intellect is usually the slave of some defunct philosopher. Mortals think by symbols, yet they are often unaware of their origins in the history of philosophy. Intellectuals who distain philosophy often assent to principles which are quite philosophical in nature. Some natural scientists speak of efficient causation or functional integration without realizing the debt they owe to Leibniz. (5)

Some mathematicians marvel at the grandeur of analytic geometry without acknowledging Descartes. (6) Secondary school teachers often assert the importance of building reasoning power without mentioning Aristotle. (7) Most Christians don't understand the Platonic influence upon Christianity.

The symbols men live by control the direction of their lives. Man is a symbolic animal. (8) Symbols are more than words, gestures, expressions or representations of something else. They come to embody their referent in a transcendent manner and allow for the comprehension of phenomena which cannot be pointed to. Above all, this is true of the self. As I look within myself by introspection, I use symbols to interpret myself. The greater the range or complexity of the symbols used, the more profound will be the examination of the 'map' of 'my being'. This is true freedom as that 'map' may be altered.

Philosophers are now as gods. They invent ideas which can examine and then transform their inner self. Whether of saint or moral monster, an emergent consciousness will be discerned. A deed-act which is needed of all social movements. (9) Now, philosophers can transform the world. If you disagree, consider the impact of the writings of Thomas Paine or Karl Marx. (10) This is the symbol of totality which will personify the thinker after death. Indeed, he will be more alive than dead. Symbols are the holy or the prime potency.

Philosophers Define the Significant

Second, the intensive study of philosophy acquaints one with the most significant issues or questions enveloping the human experience. Questions of truth, beauty, wisdom, art, freedom, equality, ideal government, goodness and the sublime among others. These queries have a noble and illuminating capacity to lift one to a higher level of conceptual understanding.

To a degree, they negate the trivial or inconsequential through which the world is darkened. (11) They prevent man from becoming dead wood. This is done when the small becomes the large and the large is reduced in size or significance.

As such, the study of the great philosophers lifts us above the sewer of the rabble to a higher cognitive awareness or apperception. It also negates the strict chain of causal determination which dominates the lower level of our organic being as it does in the vast inorganic world. Material causation cannot explain philosophical thinking which is a symbolic unity close to, yet not the same as, Jung's ideas on synchronicity. (12) The vast complex of abstractions as conceived in a philosopher's mind, in their infinite combinations or permutations, modifies, redirects or negates the bonds of material causation, functional integration or the rudimentary assumptions of behaviorist methodology. (13) Behaviorist methodology only applies to simple formats and can never explain the great ideas of beauty or truth. Great ideas are not connected materially in any causative or functional manner.

The mind of a Whitehead, a McEwen, or a Kant demonstrates a 'leap to freedom'. The highest realms of abstract thinking negate the bondage of inheritance. This is the arch of freedom, of the sublime or the holy. It is what is most sacred-the imperfect perfection or the foundation of human transcendence. Here we negate the past and the sewer of impure causation to render some contribution, however small, to our human destiny. (14) Yet, we must be careful for this is also the seat of terror. This is the realm of Marat. When we transcend our limitations or our finitude in this way, even briefly, we may become not merely saints, but also moral monsters. Augustine and

Hitler are two ends of the same spectrum. As Santayana wrote, to slay a monster one must become a monster. (15)

In impure causation, everything depends on what is antecedent or subsequent and independent or dependent as variables. But, this does not apply to the highest realms of thought. One idea does not affect another in terms of time sequences. Divergent ideas may be in the mind at the same moment and they do not affect each other materially or in terms of psychological stimuli.

Phenomena perceived forty years before may in memory affect action at this instant or goals we project onto the future may influence us now. Ideas are not atoms or electrical impulses even if brain activity is measured by electrical impulses on a machine.

If brain impulses are being measured while I think of the grand idea of liberty which is then correlated with certain electrical phenomena, this does not mean that the conception of liberty is an electrical impulse or reducible to one. The latter is the latrine of energy; the former is an ideal to die for.

An idea, by the way, does not contain what might be called the 'stuff of the universe'. It is an empty illumination. It has no substance, yet it generates the knowledge of all substance. Above all, of the self.

Philosophy Advances Science

Third, philosophy provides us with a framework for significant advances in the sciences. By bold and creative thinking, philosophers have often transcended their limited intellectual heritage to put forward bold, innovative insights that have at times shocked their compatriots. Will Durant called philosophy the front trench in the pursuit of truth. (16) It will forever be so.

Science is different from philosophy, yet the two have affected each other, or should we say, infected. Leibniz and Schopenhauer postulated the unconscious or the irrational in their metaphysical systems influencing the science of psychology. Locke also influenced cognitive psychology. Hobbes developed powerful ideas concerning the development of the national state which clearly were preliminary of sociology. Heidegger made contributions to the science of architecture. (17)

Yet, the influence goes beyond this. Philosophy offers a theoretical basis for the analysis of a specific branch of knowledge. Hence, we have a philosophy of art, of science or of social science each of which is a highly developed enterprise with an extensive literature.

(As an existential affirmation, a good part of my education consisted of studying philosophy of social science at Hofstra University under the supervision of William McEwen. During the majesty of our conversations, we discussed the theoretical basis of several diverse social sciences.

 One assumption underlying all of them is that there is an objective world to which our epistemological concepts refer. I later came to realize that this assumption needed severe scrutiny since we never know of an objective world which is 'out there', but only observe phenomena which are bodily orientated. This is true of sociology, psychology and political science.

The same is also true of the natural sciences as even the stars observed in astronomy must be interpreted bodily as per the brain and eye. Information from machines must also be processed in a similar manner. In this mode, the so-called objective world of knowledge is dependent upon the transient juxtapositions of bodily structures in evolutionary process.)

Philosophy Defines the Unique in Man

Forth, the great value of philosophy is that it brings forward what is unique in man. Every man has a right to dream of a transcendent existence, to cast off the burdens of this benighted planet and to let his finite 'my being' fill the nature of being. In philosophy, he can express what is unique in him. In short, what is in no other man! In this manner, philosophy is a cry that yields one basic message: namely, my existence counts and must be included in the history of being. (18) Being, of course, as reduced always to 'my being'.

Philosophy Enhances Existential Liberation

Fifth, philosophy is a catalyst to existential liberation. In this sense, philosophy brings about social change, either revolutionary or evolutionary. As noted previously, Enlightenment philosophers influenced the course of the French Revolution just as the utopian socialists advanced modern ideas on the economic rights of workers. Mental liberation remains an essential prerequisite for physical liberation. The success of a social movement, such as the women's movement, clearly depends upon the creation of an insurgent consciousness or a new vision of existence which, along with other factors, must eventually lead to physical freedom. (19) The absence of philosophy is for the same reason a prerequisite for enslavement.

It is important to interpret yourself. If you fail to do so, you leave open the possibility of being labeled or defined by others often resulting in negative consequences. As an example, as long as women allowed themselves to be defined by men, they were often reduced to the status of housewives. The ideas of the feminists were, in this regard, a necessary condition for female liberation.

In a similar way, as long as homosexuals allowed themselves to be defined as mentally ill, they suffered adverse consequences. The ideas of the leaders of the Gay Rights Movement were again a catalyst to their liberation and to a novel self-image of an acceptable life-style conductive to civil rights.

Philosophy reduces the potency of fanaticism. A fanatic is someone with no balance in his thinking. (20) He acts on the basis of a few unreflective principles which he obeys with simian satisfaction and worm-like simplicity. The counterweight is complex philosophical thought which is a conduit to a more balanced world-view. Philosophy remains the greatest shield against tyranny and fanaticism ever devised. Clearly, this is why tyrants hate philosophers.

1. Jellinek, Georg, The Declaration of the Rights of Man and of the Citizens, Jefferson Publications, USA, 2016.

2. Bernstein, R.B., Thomas Jefferson, Oxford, NY, 2003, pgs. 15-36.

3. Hendrix, Scott, H., Martin Luther: Visionary Reformer, Yale University Press, New Haven, 201.5.

4. Shirer, William, L., The Rise and Fall of the Third Reich: A History of Nazi Germany, Simon & Schuster, NY, 2010, pgs. 80-116.

5. Leibniz, G.W., Philosophical Essays, trans. by Roger Arlew & Daniel Gerber, Hackett Publishing, IN, 1989.

6. Descartes, Rene, The Geometry of Rene Descartes, trans. by David Eugene Smith & Marcia L. Latham, Dover, NY, 1954.

7. Aristotle, The Basic Works of Aristotle, ed. by Richard McKeon, Random House, NY, 1941, pgs. 7-216.

8. Cassirer, Ernst, The Philosophy of Symbolic Forms, Vol. 4, ed. by John Michael Krols & Donald P. Verene, trans. by John Michael Krols, Yale University press, New Haven, 1996, pgs. 34-114.

9. Staggenborg, Suzanne, Social Movements, Oxford, NY, 2016.

10. Paine, Thomas, Common Sense, Dover Publications, NY, 1997.

11. Heidegger, Martin, The Question Concerning Modern Technology and Other Essays, trans. by William Lovitt, Garland Publication, 1977.

12. Jung, C.G., Synchronicity: An Acausal Connecting Principle, trans. by R.F.C. Hull, Routledge, NY, 2010.

13. McEwen, William, Enduring Satisfaction, Philosophical Library, NY, 1949.

14. Ibid.

15. Santayana, George, The Life of Reason, Prometheus Books, NY, 1998.

16. Durant, Will, The Story of Philosophy, Simon & Schuster, NY, 1961, pg. xxvi.

17. Sharr, Adam, Heidegger for Architects, Routledge, NY, 2007, pgs. 36-95.

18. Della, Edward, The Apocalypse, Vize, NY, 2004.

19. Spinoza, Benedict, Ethics, ed. & trans, by Edwin Curley, Penguin Books, 1996, pgs. 113-169.

20. Delia, Edward, The Apocalypse, Vize Publications, NY, 2004, pg. 43.

PART TWO

Chapter 5
What Makes Philosophy Unique?

In discussing the uniqueness of philosophy, we need not repeat intellectual issues which have already been discussed. Thus, we can dismiss the suggestions that philosophy is unique in that it is the queen of the sciences or that it, unlike other disciplines, constantly encourages critical discussion. Again, philosophy is not a science and can never be a science. In addition, many fields besides philosophy constantly encourage critical analysis. There are, however, several important suggestions concerning the uniqueness of philosophy which necessitate commentary.

Philosophy Requires Mega Abstractions

While many disciplines are quite abstract, it is claimed that philosophy is abstract in a unique manner. Abstractions can be found in history, mathematics, science and many other disciplines, yet philosophical abstractions transcend them in the sense that they are more creative, more the result of the imagination and are often free from the constraints of validity, logical consistency, empirical verification or quantification.

A scientist cannot completely deny the necessity of describing the operations of an independent reality, but a philosopher can deny that there is an independent reality. A mathematician cannot totally ignore the so-called laws of mathematical inference or the 'law of contradiction', yet a philosopher can negate both.

Metaphysical concepts such as substance or being are free from any arbitrary restraints and are the result of pure intellectual deliberation. A philosopher may even go beyond the conventional sanity to speak of the unity of opposites, dream illusions or worlds dominated by the white wolf. 'My being' devours all axioms, norms, postulates or posits to create a universe of pure negation. A hole in the wall for the less than sane.

The existentialists, of course, have always understood that the 'laws of logic' cannot explain fully the meaning of human existence. (1) Human beings are not calculating machines in that they do not abide either by the 'laws of logic' or the norms of consistency. As stated previously, one, two, three- this is arithmetic, not life. One, two, three-this cannot give us the will to live. If personified, one, two, three would be a traitor to existence. An evil omen to be shunned.

Philosophical abstractions are often not tied to or limited by any historical stipulations as in the case of mathematics or in the sciences. This relative absence of limitation allows for greater creativity or redefinition which is rare anywhere else except in philosophy. It also is the reason for the lack of progress in the discipline. Life, organic being and the necessity to asset our organic existence, are the key to the meaning of any abstraction in philosophy. The content is simply that which is in 'my being' and an existential 'my being' at that- one that has a definite genesis and organic negation. It is an empty abstraction with concrete significance.

The complexity of these normless, broad-based abstractions is the ultimate reason why intense philosophical thought breaks free from the chain of natural causation or functional integration which restricts the vast bulk of our organic being. The endless permutations or combinations of these broad abstract notions combined with their empty, yet existential meaning unbound by historical roots, allows us to make a 'leap to freedom'. This is true nobility.

The prime mover. Unbound by the tyranny of determination, we make some contribution, however small, to our own creative destiny. (2) This contribution at times results in insanity, yet sanity is not a prerequisite for philosophy. Existential, empty abstract assertion is. On this foundation, the universalization of 'my being' shines as an objectification of pure, creative ego. C.I. Lewis referred to philosophy as a 'primary act of abstraction'. (3) In the above sense, it is.

Ironically, art and music are closest to philosophy in regard to its abstract content being normless. Only in regard to the production is a great painter limited by conventional norms or procedures, but not in regard to the content or intended message which he desires to convey. In production, a painter is limited by his art materials, techniques of color coordination or appropriate methods of design, perspective or the depiction of light among other concerns.

He must learn these techniques in order to adequately generate a work of art. He is in Heidegger's sense 'thrown' into an already existing world which is historically conditioned. A world which is a realm of interest, concern or desire. If an artist lived in the 13th Century, he probably would use egg tempera on wood, poplar or oak.

In the 15th Century, he likely would use oil. In this sense, we are all creatures of technology. Yet, once a painting is produced, the content or intended message of an artist may be a pure projection of his 'my being' without any reference to the historical past of the race. His unique existence, his novel way of looking at the world or what is in him as in no other being who has ever conceived - this is the mega-vision! A titan against a titan! The negation of all which is external. The devouring of pure being into nothingness as 'my being' universalizes.

Now, this is not meant to deny that the ideas conveyed in art have been historically determined and often they have been. The point is that they do not necessarily have to be as these ideas are not bound to any norms. Production cannot be devoid of norms or the artist would convey nothing. In content, however, a painter may express anything no matter how absurd or unrealistic.

He is not bound to describe an independent reality unless he desires to. He may ignore the conventional world of ideas and project only what is in him. He may universalize his inner being. He may be realistic such as Rembrandt or a master of fantasy such as Rousseau. (4) He may render social commentary such as Hogarth or mythology as in the case of Titian. (5) A magical world devoid of movement or a planet dominated by the white wolf may all be conveyed in a painting. In the 20th Century, even productive techniques have departed from norms as in the case of abstract art and in movements such as Cubism.

The same can be said of music at least in terms of the masterpieces of the great composers. The genesis of music is limited in production only, but not in content or the intended message. In production, music is limited by the instruments in addition to 'proper' musical theory and score, yet in intended message music may convey any meaning whatsoever including those which transcend conventional ideas or socially accepted norms.

In the end, philosophical abstractions are greater than any other. They are mega-abstractions capable of integrating all other abstractions formulated in diverse disciplines into a systematic cathedral of insight. Now, every individual 'my being' is 'thrown' back into the world of total being as a retaliation for having been 'thrown' into this benighted world in the first place. We attack being- itself in revenge for our finitude. Yet, in truth we attack nothing as being- itself is nothing. The attempt, however, beings a temporary relief as a cry to all being that my being has existed and will be recognized.

In this sense, philosophy is a cry or a plea to the totality of being for attention. (6) Beyond this, such a cathedral of mega-abstractions provides a portal of illumination into the nature of 'my being', not as a category in Whitehead's sense as all categories are enveloped within the imperfect structure of language, but rather as a deed-act which exists beyond the rational in an existential mode. This cathedral is in no sense a subset of the totality as phenomenal categories, in fact, are a subset of metaphysical modes. Rather, the cathedral is an index of humanity and ultimately of the entire human symbolic universe.

Philosophy as Devoid of Presuppositions

Philosophy has been idealized as a unique method where no presupposition is sacrosanct. In short, where no assumption, either overt or covert, is beyond scrutiny. Philosophers constantly must examine received opinions or underlying axioms and, in this sense, liberate mankind from ignorance. This idea is clearly in the Socratic tradition.

While this is true to a certain extent, it is definitely not unique or specific to philosophy. Physicists also question underlying assumptions as Einstein did in his reinterpretation of time. Likewise, mathematicians are keen in this regard as can be discerned by examining the development of non-Euclidean geometry which contradicted the conventional wisdom concerning space.

In general, it should be noted that questioning presuppositions is functional only to a limited degree. Uncontrolled, continuous questioning or doubt may be disruptive to intelligent reflection or dialogue. It may also lead to a solipsism which no one except dysfunctional philosophers or madmen take seriously. All intelligent reflection rests upon unit assumptions or axioms which are accepted on the basis of what Santayana calls 'animal faith'. (7)

While intelligent reflection requires the scrutiny of some key assumptions, a total, endless questioning of all axioms is merely a sign of a weak, dysfunctional mind. In regard to doubt, a philosophical statute of limitations is necessary. Only in this manner may we avoid the black hole of solipsism and emerge into the realm of reflective transcendence.

While philosophy offers a broad range of academic freedom in regard to intelligent doubt, it would be a mistake to stretch this freedom beyond a reasonable point. Since philosophy is broader in scope and has no definite delineated subject matter, a philosopher must know when doubt is appropriate and when aimless questioning must cease.

This capacity speaks more of an art than a science and usually comes after long, reflective thought. The capacity is, however, not entirely rational in nature. Notice Spinoza's occasional unwillingness to answer continuous, unwarranted questions in his learned correspondence. (8)

'I Know Nothing'- Socrates

In what is thought to be the Socratic tradition, philosophy is believed to be unique in that it supposedly truly demonstrates the depth of our ignorance. Socrates is quoted as saying, "I know nothing". This assertion is believed to be the tabernacle of wisdom. The reasoning is as follows. As we critically examine philosophical issues, we gain increasing insight into the limits of our knowledge and the unlimited capacity of our vanity. This realization is believed to be of vital significance in the pursuit of philosophical acumen.

Now, this contention is good as far as it goes and unfortunately it does not go far. First, many scholars deny that Socrates actually said this and question the sources cited in support of this quotation. (9)

Even if the quote is verified, there is doubt as to what he meant by the assertion.

In Plato's dialogues, Socrates does assert that he knows certain things such as his assertions while he was dying. (10) There is an apparent contradiction here if one believes in the 'law of contradiction". By the way, if you know nothing, how can you know that you know nothing? We will not attempt to resolve these issues here as tempting as it is to provide an effort.

Secondly, one does not need philosophy to demonstrate the depths of human ignorance. A five minute conversation with a politician would do as well; The depths of human ignorance and stupidity are quite obvious, universal, directly evident and deplorable.

While philosophical study may bring one a more sophisticated view of this phenomenon, it is not necessary for its initial realization. Even in respect to your own realization of the limits of your knowledge, it is doubtful if philosophy helps much here either. Psychological factors are more responsible for unrestrictive egoism than intellectual ones. Moreover, many other academic disciplines may direct the mind into maturity in regard to reasonable doubt concerning common knowledge.

(As an existential affirmation, the following insight might be of value. When it comes to their own ideas, philosophers are often quite assertive or dogmatic and in no manner do they believe that they are ignorant or engaged in folly. It would be inappropriate to mention a detailed list of names and I do not exclude myself, yet some names may be noted. Hume, the great skeptic, seems to be assured of the vitality of his own intellect. Spinoza is often quite convinced of the truth or logical correctness of his philosophy. Kant probably would object if he were included in the ranks of the ignorant.

Just in passing, philosophers should not look down on the ignorant. In a sense, we all are ignorant of certain things and none is above folly. Clowns, drunkards and idiots serve many purposes. They remind us of our own folly, they make life more interesting and they have a tendency to tell the truth when wise men will not. They also provide motivation to others to rise above bland stupidity. They provide most of us with job security. A world devoid of idiots would be a world without laughter.)

Philosophy as a Preparation for Death

Philosophy is often thought to be unique in that it provides a potent preparation for death. This is an interesting perspective and is clearly illustrated by the death of Socrates as presented by Plato. (11) Socrates faced death with acceptance, self-possession and magnanimity as a consequence of his decision to obey the laws of the city-state of Athens whose leaders had decreed his death. Hume also faced death with self-possession and acceptance. (12) There is little reason to doubt that Spinoza had peace of mind and tranquility when he faced life's final calamity.

This view might be true, yet there is room for doubt. Socrates' absence of fear may have had little to do with philosophical reflection. In his younger days, Socrates was a hoplite warrior and engaged in brutal front line battle for Athens. (13)

It is probable that he never had much fear in him since a hoplite warrior had to be prepared for brutal death at any time. Different people react to death in diverse ways depending upon temperament and the nature of each individual's 'my being': that is, of one's inner self.

This has little to do with intellect as 'my being' and 'my death' are related. 'My being' is not merely a rational construct, but rather is a consequence of the irrational as well. There is no universal formula which may erase the fear of facing death as each man must encounter it alone.

Philosophers have often differed as to the meaning of death. Epictetus wrote that death is nothing to us. (14) Wittgenstein asserted that death is not an event in life. (15) Heidegger believed that death sets a limit to life and enhances its meaning. (16) He also interprets death as the key to understanding life. These statements exhibit wisdom, yet they neither explain death nor prepare us for its calamity. There are no experts on death. Even if there were, the explanation of death in general would be irrelevant to me. It is 'my death' that is significant as 'my death' is different than anybody else's death.

In Heidegger's terms, 'my death' means that I am no longer in the world. Thus, the question of finitude becomes paramount and the meaning of my existence emerges as the most significant issue which reduces all others in size.

Death in general and 'my death' are quite disparate, Death in general is a biological necessity and is often viewed as a natural end. 'My death' is viewed, with few exceptions, as a calamity, as are the deaths of my significant others. Death in general provides for social change and prevents man from living forever in his own corruption.

It also allows for the redistribution of wealth and power. Yet, very few would think of their own demise in this manner. 'My death' erases my existence and studying philosophy cannot reverse that odious fact. (As an existential affirmation, let me say that it is absurd to fear death. No matter how afraid you are, you still have to die. I see no glory in death as any slob may expire. It is life that requires a plan, a vision or a determination of will to accomplish whatever one must accomplish. This is the affirmation of my will.

One more thing. As horrible as death is, it possesses one great quality; namely, everyone must expire! In this world of massive inequality, this is the one supreme equality. As I look back upon my past, it causes me no great pain that every benighted individual I've ever known must die!)

Philosophy as a Substitute for Religion

* As related to the above issue, it is often asserted that philosophy provides a substitute for religion. This view was particularly prevalent in the 20th Century when Marxism and Nazism were thought to be religious substitutes. Both failed miserably. Before that, Spinoza's metaphysical system was regarded in the same manner as were many others. Yet despite these attempts, religion was not displaced and continued to expand.

The reason is that religion is founded on irrational motivations to a much greater extent than philosophy is. Religion's ultimate purpose is to connect man's puny existence with some great sacred principle. The motivation is irrational and cannot be understood entirely through reason. Santayana's remark is worthy of repeating. He noted that philosophers have rarely found god while the faithful have never lost sight of him. (17) Faith is equal to reason despite the modern preference for the latter.

In truth, religion envelops more than god. God is a Western concept to be found mainly in Judaism, Christianity or Islam, yet Buddhism in pure form is non-theistic as are many third world faiths. Durkheim correctly defined religion as the realm of the holy which is the opposite of the profane. (18) The holy evokes awe or purity in an amoral world.

Philosophy can never replace religion since it can never provide or substitute for the vital societal functions which religion has. Religion is a universal and appears in all societies whether primitive, medieval or modern. There may be individuals who claim to be without faith, but there is no society without religious phenomena.

Even in Paleolithic times, graves have been uncovered which clearly have no pragmatic, but rather a ceremonial function. (19) In religion, man seems to be searching for something greater than can be found in this life. It's almost as if each individual's being is reaching for an eternal which cannot be touched. Yet, the major faiths and especially Christianity provide us with the assurance that death is not final.

Very few possess sufficient intellect to live without the mystic assumptions and ritualistic practices found in religion. After all, a funeral is for the living, not the dead. The purpose of a funeral is to allow the moral community to surround the family or friends and provide empathy or suggestions of metaphysical transcendence in order for the functions of social life to continue with minimal interference. It is doubtful that a philosopher at such a ceremony would be a worthy substitute for a priest.

Religion also serves other functions. It often provides the backbone for mores which ensure the basis of our sense of good and evil. These mores are quite different than any ethical philosophy since they are a consequence of societal forces or irrational pragmatic sequences over myriads of years which are then passed down from one generation to another. Philosophers may evaluate mores, yet never has an individual rational philosophy, such as utilitarianism or deontology, replaced them. Mores are social facts which constrain individual ethical behavior. (20) Singular, individualistic ethical theories are a matter of personal preference despite any rational efforts to universalize them.

Social order is another function of religion creating a sense of social identity or social status. As philosophers are for the most part solitary individuals, no philosophy, with the exceptions of Marxism or Nazism, could substitute for this function. Even in these isolated cases, religion in Russia or Germany was not eradicated. In Communist Cuba, it is noteworthy that Pope Francis visited Cuba in 2015 and was received with enthusiasm.

Mythology is a final function and has been described by Schopenhauer as 'poor man's metaphysics'. Mythology attempts to answer questions which science or common sense cannot. Why should anything exist at all? What is the purpose of existence?

Wittgenstein put it best when he wrote that the meaning of the world must lie outside the world. (21) Wittgenstein's world is the world of descriptive facts and we must render assumptions or point to possible realities beyond this world in order to properly describe it. This may be done rationally in philosophy, but most men know too little of this discipline for it to appeal to them let alone to replace the functions of an established mythology as found in the Bible.

In the end, the meaning of life may exist on two levels. First, on the basis of the divine inspiration. Second, as per reflection in the human realm. Both are necessary and may at times reinforce each to. They remain, however, disparate in form and function.

A Cathedral of Illumination

The ultimate uniqueness of philosophy is the establishment of a cathedral of illumination where mega-abstractions relate every singular 'my being' the totality of being. The cathedral would render the divine order, the social order and the natural order intelligible in a manner not possible in any specific discipline alone. Within it, the techniques of the natural and social sciences would be utilized in addition to the methods of pure mathematics, the ideas of religion, the arts and the history of philosophy.

It is not, however an objective categorical analysis such as Whitehead's as there is no assumption here that every element of human experience may be interpreted. Phenomenal categories such as space, time, motion, quality, cause or number cannot be assumed to be descriptive of the entire symbolic universe. Phenomenal categories only pertain to 'my being' as that self relates to the totality. The totality which is metaphysical remains a mystery.

Everything I know relates to 'my being' including my interpretation of the world. 'My world' and 'my being' are one. The quest of my philosophy is to go beyond 'my being in order to seek what is true of the symbolic universe. Postulated relations between the divine order, the social order and the natural order is the key to insight.

The cathedral envisions a phenomenological metaphysics which combines two disciplines which are thought to be exclusive of each other. It envelops autobiography in addition, to the more historical concerns as listed above. Above all, it mandates the existential affirmation as the inclusion of the inner self in all objective reports. Man is not a series of categories. He may transcend them and this may be his destiny.

1. Kaufman, Walter, Existentialism from Dostoevsky to Sartre, Penguin, NY, 1975, pgs. 280-374.

2. McEwen, William, Enduring Satisfaction, Philosophical Library, NY, 1949.

3. C.I. Lewis, Mind and the World Order: Outline of a Theory of Knowledge, Dover, NY, 1956, pgs. 1-35.

4. Rembrandt, Self-Portrait at 34, National Gallery, London, 1640; Rousseau, Surprised, National Gallery, London, 1891.

5. Titan, Bacchus and Ariadne, National Gallery, London, 1520-23; Hogarth, Marriage A-La Mode: 2, National Gallery, London, 1743.

6. Delia, Edward, The Apocalypse, Vize, NY, 2004.

7. Santayana, George, Skepticism and Animal Faith: Introduction to a System of Philosophy, Dover, NY, 1955.

8. Spinoza, Baruch, Ethics and Selected Letters, ed. by Seymour Feldman, Hackett Publishing Co., IN, 1992, pgs. 263-293.

9. Tavlor. C.W. Socrates, Oxford, University Press, 1998, pg. 46.

10. Plato, Five Dialogues, trans. G.E.M. Grube, Hackett Publishing, IN, 2002, pgs. 21-44.

11. Ibid.

12. Harris, James, A., Hume: An Intellectual Biography, Cambridge University Press, NY, 2015, pgs. 461-472.

13. Harl, Kenneth, W., The Peloponnesian War, The Teaching Co., VA, 2007.

14. Epictetus, Enchiridion, ed. by Tom Crawford, Dover, NY, 2004.

15. Wittgenstein, Ludwig, Tractatus Logico-Philosophicus, trans. C.K. Ogden, Dover, NY, 1999. Prop. 6.4311.

16. Heidegger, Martin, Being and Time, trans. by John Macquarrirl & Edward Robinson, Harper & Row, NY, 2008.

17. Santayana, George, The Life of Reason: Reason in Religion, Dover, NY, 1982.

18. Durkheim, Emile, The Elementary Forms of Religious Life, trans.by Karen E. Fields, The Free Press, NY, 1999, pgs. 303-329.

19. Wunn, Ina & Grojnowski, Davina, Ancestors, Territoriality and Gods: A Natural History of Religion, Springer, Berlin, 2016.

20. Brinkerhoff, David, & Weitz, Rose, & Ortega, Suzanne, Essentials of Sociology, 9TH Edition, Wadsworth, CA, 2014, pg. 39.

21. Wittgenstein, Ludwig, Tractatus Logico-Philosophicus, trans. C.K. Ogden, Dover, NY 1999. Prop. 6.41.

Chapter 6
Miscellaneous Considerations

Imagination in Philosophy

As with all concepts, the meaning of the term imagination has changed over time. Hobbes believed that it was simply a decaying image, Kant believed that it was vital to the understanding and Deleuze believed that it was a creative capacity. The Romantic poets had already advanced the creative idea.

In this sense, it is often believed that imagination is vital to philosophy. After all, philosophers have at times advanced imaginative conjectures. Imagination consists of many factors including the ability to visualize what is not, to explore juxtapositions among ideas not usually related and the boldness to suggest unrealized possibilities of human transcendence. Many philosophers have exhibited a powerful creative imagination, yet this capacity is clearly not specific to philosophy. Artists, musicians, poets, scientists, historians among others have at times displayed a soaring imagination. Nonetheless, a sizable amount of philosophical literature displays the summit of imaginative, speculative conjecture.

Philosophy in this respect is similar to fiction and this is the reason why an adequate philosophical education should include fictional formats such as short stories, plays, novels, poems and historical fiction. Powerful insights can be located in the work of Kafka, Shakespeare, Masters, Shelley, Hardy, Tolstoy or Dickens. A mind bereft of these great writers is demeaned.

A creative imagination is vital to a philosopher's mission to provide novel insights or unrealized visions, to open up unresolved mysteries or novel avenues of discourse enhancing the hope of human transcendence. The cathedral of illumination is as much a product of the imagination as it is of reason or the autobiography of the singular thinker. Mega-abstractions cannot be generated by reason alone, but rather by 'my being' which includes imaginative conjectures which soar high and with distinction.

The Best Medium for Philosophical Expression

The best medium for philosophical discussion depends on the nature of the manuscript and the subject area of interest. Obviously, a short publication of less than fifty pages on a delimited topic or a 'pastry chef' article would be best presented in a philosophical journal. A detailed treatise such as Kant's critical philosophy would be more adequately expressed in a learned book. Yet, not many philosophers have this type of intense, systematic mind and might prefer to write shorter articles on critical issues.

While asserting this, let it be understood that there is no attempt here to demean shorter essays which appear in scholarly journals. Some of the most significant contributions to 20th Century philosophy have originated in this fashion. There is, however, one great negative about journals, hardly politic, which should be noted. Some journals are simply mechanisms to enhance the careers of those who founded them. Some have, also, been quite partial in giving priority to the research of faculty members connected with the university or institute which subsidizes the periodical. This type of favoritism places non-academic considerations ahead of intellectual merit. The reader should himself consider the implications of this and hopefully will judge it in a spirit of intellectual honesty or self-scrutiny.

One further comment is in order. Good reference books are necessary in this field and the greatest is the one produced by Paul Edwards in 1967 which has been since updated. (1) Not only is it a detailed source of information on nearly all vital philosophical issues, but it also contains articles which are in themselves original contributions to the discipline. It is the best philosophical database in the English language.

The Best Society for Philosophical Development

Under ideal conditions, philosophy is supposed to soar best in an open society based on democratic principles. The rationale is that great ideas should be open to public debate or intellectual scrutiny devoid of government interference or censorship. The summit of democracy is often thought to be Ancient Athens where the general will of all citizens reigned supreme in the Athenian Assembly.

There are, however, several problems with this contention. First, in Ancient Athens, Socrates was put to death for corrupting the youth. While this occurred during a period when democratic institutions were undermined, it still occurred in Athenian society. Second, great philosophical traditions have been established in societies with authoritarian governments such as Germany or Russia. Despite long periods of authoritarian rule, Germany gave the world Leibniz, Kant, Hegel, Schopenhauer, Nietzsche and Heidegger. As for Russia, the name Tolstoy seals the argument.

The need to philosophize is essential to the human spirit and no government, authoritarian or otherwise, can suppress it. In his political writings, Spinoza argued that the human mind is the most difficult of our entire being to control. (2) In this sense, philosophy will flourish regardless of the form of government.

By the way, authoritarian governments are not the only ones who attempt to discredit, control or censor philosophical thought. Democratic institutions can also suppress ideas. Consider the harsh treatment of Bertrand Russell at the City College of New York or the ostracism of Spinoza during the 17th Century in a democratic environment. (3)

Robert Merton has written powerfully of what he calls the 'Mathew Effect'. (4) The idea derives from the Gospel of Saint Mathew who describes the effect of being favored by the Almighty. In Merton's context, it refers to certain social classes, schools of thought, institutions or individuals who receive preferential treatment. As an example, faculty members from Ivy league institutions often receive priority for publication over scholars from lesser known colleges. During the 20th Century which exhibited the height of the analytic movement, works on analytic philosophy or logic gained priority for publication over books or articles on metaphysics. Of course, there were exceptions such as in the case of the 'Review of Metaphysics'. (5) All of this clearly represents a form of bias and an unintentional form of censorship. Censorship intertwined with our so-called democratic way of life.

Philosophy as a Vocation

Is philosophy a vocation? Is it similar to a religious order or a secret society? Pythagoras clearly thought so. (6) As for Karl Mannheim, he suggested that the role of philosopher arose out of the earlier role of the sage or magician in primitive society. (7) Admittedly, it is common for a great philosopher to be referred to as a sage.

These ideas, however, are absurd. First, most philosophers do not have any clearly discernible religious beliefs and regard magic as a relic of an uncivilized past. Secondly, a religious order usually mandates a prescribed code of ethics which is enforced by sanctions and no such code exists in the greater philosophical community. Third, the sage, magician or shaman is often given a high or respected place in their designated communities. Philosophers today are often treated as lowly members of the socio-economic order. In America, they are usually treated as rubbish. Fourth, the sage is commonly the elder of the tribe who displays wisdom concerning life's joys or tragedies. Philosophers today often discuss technical matters concerning language which is of little concern to ordinary citizens and is likely to be looked upon by them as useless chatter. Fifth, the sage, magician or shaman usually interacts within a primary group setting whereas thinkers in modern times rarely do so and are generally associating within secondary groups. Finally, there is no hard empirical evidence that the status of philosopher is usually related to the status of the sage as a matter of anthropological reference. For all these reasons, the ideas of Pythagoras and Mannheim must be rejected.

A related question, in connection with Pythagoras, is whether philosophical groups constitute what could be called secret societies. This is possible, yet highly improbable. Pythagoras' community might be referred to in this manner and so could the Marxist philosophical cells in Russia in 1917. But this is relatively rare. Philosophical associations or clubs today are simply organizations or groups to promote the development or exchange of ideas. They are open to wide participation among scholars and can in no manner be described as secret societies.

There has, however, been one attempt to render the entire discipline of philosophy secret in the sense of separating its intellectual riches from the common mass of mankind. Centuries ago, there was an attempt to render Latin as the official language of philosophical expression. There is no implication here that this was the consequence of a conspiracy of specific individuals. It was probably more of a social trend or a philosophical folkway which prevailed for a time. In any case, numerous books were written in Latin which most citizens could not understand since Latin is a dead language and was usually only learned in universities. One of these books was Spinoza's famous treatise on ethics. The reasoning behind this trend was in part that the common masses do not have the intellect to evaluate bold philosophical ideas with tolerance.

This reasoning is erroneous. To erect a barrier between the common masses and the great ideas is the equivalent of reducing the masses to philosophical ignorance. Philosophy must not become a haven for the elect. Men need to philosophize and women too. They need to understand the great questions of existence. Common citizens have noble dreams and unique visions as well as the professional. The mission of philosophy must be one of openness to the greater mass of humanity. Books and journals should be accessible to the common citizen. Philosophy is an achievement of culture and a culture devoid of philosophy is a marginal one.

The Best Training in Philosophy

In Ancient Athens, learning philosophy from a master such as Plato would have been the preferred way. Today, earning a graduate degree in philosophy form a college or university would be the usual manner. It is doubtful, however, whether any reflective person would confine himself to either alternative.

There is no single path to philosophical wisdom. Aquinas and Melbranche studied theology. Epictetus was a slave. Spinoza grinded and polished lenses. Wittgenstein was an engineer and Whitehead mastered mathematical physics. A thousand paths lead to philosophy.

Philosophers have never been judged historically on the basis of degrees earned or academic positions held, but rather by the power of their ideas, or what they believed in and the values they embraced. The important matter was how they operated their minds or expressed their insights and the conviction they displayed even when fearful. Fear is not a philosophy, yet fear has dictated many woeful philosophies.

Of course, there are some basics in learning philosophy. The first would be mastering the history of the discipline and reading the most significant classics. Second, experiencing several major sub-divisions of the field such as metaphysics, logic, ethics, aesthetics, epistemology in addition to a study of philosophy of science or social science. Of course, other concerns may be included as well. Third, private, continuous discussions with a master of philosophy is essential to sharpen one's ideas. It does not necessarily have to be a student-teacher interaction, yet it should be supervised by someone with philosophical expertise. Dialectics is vital in philosophy. Thomas Aquinas wrote dialectically.

(As an existential affirmation, I was extremely fortunate in this regard. At Hofstra University, Dr. William McEwen was the Dean of Faculty and had the rare privilege to hold individual one-on-one courses with graduate students. I took several courses with him between 1974 and 1977 and this individual attention over years led me to an understanding which could not be attained in a large classroom. McEwen was a student of Alfred North Whitehead and had his doctoral dissertation supervised by Whitehead. He also expanded upon Whitehead's philosophy in two learned books. The major topic of our discussions was philosophy of social science and I owe him a great debt.)

Progress in Philosophy

Is there progress in philosophy? This is an important question and the answer further demonstrates the difference between science and philosophy. Yet, what is progress? Progress denotes moving beyond or surpassing older, inadequate theories or ideas and replacing them with new, more adequate or comprehensive ones in terms of deductive or inductive inference resulting in greater predictive or explanatory value.

Now, no reflective person would deny that there has been progress in physics since Aristotle wrote his learned treatise on the subject. (8) Yet, Aristotle's ideas are still considered among the best philosophy has to offer in fields as ethics, metaphysics and politics.

Beyond this, in more modern times has anyone ever surpassed the ideas of Spinoza, Leibniz or Kant? There have been different theories or refinements of older theories in addition to the invention of novel fields of philosophy. But, has anyone gone beyond their insights in the sense expressed above?

Has the quality of their ideas ever been surpassed? The answer must be a reluctant no! Despite the greatness of more modern thinkers such as Quine, Wittgenstein or Russell, the basic ideas of Plato, Aristotle, Leibniz or Kant have not been disregarded and their ideas still remain as some of the most significant contributions to the great questions of existence.

Philosophy has never exhibited progress as science has for the good and sufficient reason that philosophy is not and can never be a science. This so-called progress in science is only regarded as such by the weight of contemporary scientific consensus and is always subject to be overturned by further empirical testing or even modifications in its conceptual apparatus.

To the contrary, the history of philosophy exhibits insights which will continue endlessly in that they exist in themselves and are self-sufficient. Future. insights will not overturn their relevance or diminish their veracity.

This accumulation of insights may not exhibit progress, yet it amounts to an inventory of ideas as a human heritage. Philosophy is a humanity. In the end, philosophical insights enable a reflective person, after careful study, to gain an inkling of eternity. Above all, an inkling into the nature of his singular 'my being' and its relationship to the totality.

Philosophy and Mythology

A myth is a tale of cosmic significance which may be transmitted over decades or even centuries by oral tradition or religious inspiration. A myth is not necessarily false, yet most probably are devoid of fact. They evoke philosophical dispositions in answering queries which cannot be solved either by science or common sense. A myth only emerges in societies where there is considerable culture and, as Santayana suggested, where genius prevails. (9) This genius is poetical.

However, let it be understood that the genius here is the collective genius of the race, not of an isolated individual. The soul of mankind is expressed through myths regardless of where they appear. Carl Jung and Joseph Campbell both believed that mythology is a consequence of intense, a priori' insights which genetically transmit the heritage of the ages to successive generations. (10) Jung referred to these 'a priori' forms of thought as archetypes. (11)

To the contrary, philosophy is often the product of a series of isolated thinkers or singular individuals.

A few may be influential, yet no one person can ever represent an entire race. Despite what Hegel believed, the spirit of the age does not speak through any one of them. (12) This is the main reason why philosophy will never eliminate the need for mythology which speaks of an unconscious, collective wisdom whose meaning is beyond the grasp of any solitary thinker. Mythology informs of the heritage of the race. Philosophy conveys the creative advance of individuals.

Philosophy and Stratification

With few exceptions throughout history, philosophers have been relegated to the lowest levels of the socio-economic class structure, Despite Plato's dream of philosopher-kings, they also have had little prestige or power. The exception, of course, would be Germany during the Second Reich. (13)

There are several reasons for this. First, mankind needs nothing more than wisdom, yet desires nothing less. Herein lies the dilemma and fate of man. Second, most laymen regard philosophy as a sort of intellectual conspicuous consumption. Philosophy seems to them, to use a slang phrase, to be 'neither here nor there' and the field does not seem necessary for the productive efforts of life. Third, many believe that philosophy consists of merely giving opinions rather than being a strict academic discipline. Finally, there are a few who are intellectually incapable of comprehending the great ideas.

Being human, philosophers cannot but lament the disrespect accorded to them. This is particularly true of those who have been relegated to penury. Marx spent most of his life in poverty. Nietzsche lived in an attic and Spinoza survived by grinding or polishing lenses. Mankind's disrespect for wisdom has resulted in great philosophical masterpieces being ignored for generations. Hume's, 'A Treatise of Human Nature', and Schopenhauer's, "The World as Will and

Representation', are prime examples. In recent times, many books in philosophy have to be subsidized and it is often difficult to find a publisher: On the other hand, insignificant works on sex, gossip or even humor are rushed into print.

When foolishness becomes the mainstay of society, wisdom is banished.

In this difficult situation, philosophers must look into themselves and draw upon their inner strength and self-possession. They must remember that their wisdom will sustain them long after the foolishness of their compatriots fades into ignominy.

Philosophy and the History of Philosophy

What is the relationship between philosophy and the history of philosophy? While improbable, it is technically possible to be a great philosopher without a thorough schooling in the history of the discipline. As previously noted, Thales had a limited history available to him, yet his thinking must still be regarded as a solitary, creative advance which was quite remarkable for his time. The same could be said for the other pre-Socratic thinkers. Today, however, the intellectual tradition is so complex that it must be consulted or studied to obtain competence. Rarely is an idea truly innovative or without antecedents in the history of ideas.

All thinkers are to some extent affected by the prevailing philosophical tradition. Their mind has been shaped by it and the direction of their thinking has been charted. Their individual 'my being' may provide alternative directions and herein lies the point of intellectual courage. The courageous deed-act in which we make a small, yet significant, contribution to our own creative destiny. The deed-act that transcends any reified heritage enveloped in an unthinking, conventional accord. This deviation from that accord which served as the point of genesis provides the foundation stone of creativity.

One important note should be added. Those who create their own philosophy are not superior to the historians of philosophy. The two are interrelated. Moreover, innovative insights have often been advanced by the historian of ideas. A historian of philosophy clarifies, integrates, examines and critically reinterprets the great classics. K. T. Fann's, *Wittgenstein's Conception of Philosophy*, and John Burnet's, *Early Greek Philosophy*, are powerful examples of great historical works. (14) Also, Heidegger and Nietzsche were both great philosophers and great historians of philosophy. The former's great work was on Heraclitus; the latter's concerned Greek tragedy. (15)

Sex and Philosophy

How does sex affect a person's philosophy? Sex lies in the realm of total irrationality. It is the id or pleasure principle. Freud believed that it was the predominant instinct in man. (16) Reason.is biologically centered in the cerebrum. The cock has no cerebrum. It is blind, irrational will and the fulfillment or denial of this sex instinct may have a profound effect upon an individual's world-view. Certainly, this was true in the case of Schopenhauer and Nietzsche. One has only to examine in detail their relevant biographies to comprehend this assertion.

It can, however, be more clearly visualized by examining the rise of feminist philosophy. Women definitely have a different set of interests or world-views then men do. Some feminist thinking is a rebellion against patriarchal control, yet the bulk of it is a shift to divergent topics of more concern to women. By the way, it is untrue that women are less interested in sex than men. They are just as interested and at times even more so.

The thinking of both sexes can be polluted by sexual interest. If the human mind is dominated by the impure, irrational will for sex, then this aspect of his being must be considered to be less than rational even by conventional standards of rationality. Perhaps, as March and Simon suggested, man can only be 'intendedly rational or rational only for certain limited times-in places usually connected with organizational functioning. (17)

The influence of sex is most clearly seen in our dreams. At night, the most rational mind descends into a pit of urine, incest and madness. (18) A world of pure negation which is the nemesis of this artificial, phony world of bourgeois ideals. A world in which we attempt to crush all conventions. Debauch utopial. We commit murder at night while we dream of ideals during the day. Philosophy may be a diversion or interruption from man's quest for sexual fulfillment.

Philosophy and Genius

Genius is a capacity which can neither be predicted nor controlled. No one truly understands genius for the good and sufficient reason that the mind of the genius transcends all conventional interpretations. The rarity of genius is the reason why philosophical ideas cannot be totally determined by social-historical factors or in any manner predicted on the basis of an analysis of such factors.

Genius consists in making a relatively self-determined contribution which leads to an understanding of the great ideas. Genius is not, as Schopenhauer believed, a purely objective will to knowledge. The subjective realm, the 'my being' of the genius, is clearly involved. All purely objective facts must be interpreted within the domain of the self. An objective will to know apart from the inner realm of 'my being' is a misconception.

117

The mind of the genius must, within his inner self, analyze, integrate or rearrange disparate elements of experience into a novel vision constituting a noble chapter in the history of mankind. A genius represents what mankind can accomplish when freed from the bonds of servitude to a reified intellectual heritage. Thus, the genius serves as a shield against tyranny.

A genius is rarely understood during his lifetime since his creative imagination transcends the comprehension of those determined by the world-view enveloped in the false, bourgeois world of the commonplace. He works nót only for the present generation, but for the future of mankind. Yet, he works also for an understanding of his own inner self.

Phenomenological Metaphysics

Metaphysics is the most significant philosophical discipline. It entails the study of ultimate reality or the nature of being. Yet, all we know is phenomena and a phenomenological metaphysics is rendered paramount. This is, of course, contrary to the modern analytic tradition which decrees the 'death of metaphysics'. (19) This slogan neither negates not contradicts the truth that all philosophy lies within the domain of metaphysics.

All ideational discourse rests upon unproven principles or assumptions and the examination of them is justifiably in the realm of that discipline. We observe phenomena and then posit unproven assumptions or principles which leads us in turn to analyze their implications. The positing might not entirely be conscious, but stem from the collective unconscious.

The difficulty of providing satisfactory answers to metaphysical queries does not negate the significance of the attempt. The same would be true of any other philosophical field of interest.

Metaphysical inquiry is particularly difficult since its speculations often transcend our limited language structure. This should not, however, inhibit or cause us to cease, the process of creative thinking. Approximations of greatness are preferable to the smallness of exactitude. Engaging oneself in the profound power of the great ideas is better than mastering the infernal smallness of a limited grammatical analysis.

There is a great danger in engrossing oneself in the trivial or the inconsequential. Edgar Lee Masters put it best in describing the life of a banker whose time was engulfed by money matters and other mundane pursuits. Upon his death, these trivial concerns meant nothing to him. Masters' concludes, "How great it is to write the single line, Roll on thou deep and dark blue ocean Roll". (20)

The Implications of Metaphysical Predominance

It is necessary to entäil what metaphysical predominance means and what it does not mean. First, it does not mean that other fields of philosophy are insignificant. It does mean, however, that there are unproven ideas, principles, assumptions or methods underlying those other disciplines which fall into the domain of metaphysics.

Second, it does not entail that all of philosophy must be burdened by endless metaphysical queries, but only that philosophers must recognize the nature of this metaphysic in their interpretative dialogue. It goes without saying that there can never be a finalized philosophy of the meaning of meaning since the interpretative metaphysic underlying all conceptual or theoretical formulations would always be open to reinterpretation. As philosophical ideas are extended into new domains, the metaphysic of the meaning of meaning must be modified.

The Great Question

The great question of metaphysics is to discern what is and from this genesis all other significant questions arise. Specifically, what human nature is and what human relations ought to be. Thus, the metaphysics of knowledge follows next.

1. Edwards, Paul, (Editor-In-Chief), The Encyclopedia of Philosophy, 1st Edition, Macmillan-Collier, 1972.

2. Bento, Antonio, & Jose Rosa Silva, (Editors), Revisiting Spinoza: Theological-Political Treatise, Georg Olms Verlag, 2013.

3. Lehman, Devra, Spinoza: The Outcast Thinker, Namelos, NH, 2014, pgs-87-98.

4. Merton, Robert, K., "The Mathew Effect in Science", in Science, 159, (380), pgs. 56-63.

5. Weiss, Paul, (Founder), The Review of Metaphysics, 1947-present.

6. Kahn, Charles, H., Pythagoras and the Pythagoreans, Hackett Publishing, NY, 2001.

7. Mannheim, Karl, Ideology and Utopia: An Introduction to the Sociology of Knowledge, 1st Edition, Harvest Books, FL, 1955.

8. Aristotle, Physics, trans. by Robin Waterfield, Oxford University Press, NY, 2008.

9. Santayana, George, The Life of Reason, Or the Phrases of Human Progress: Reason in Religion, Chapter IV, BiblloBazaar, 2009.

10. Jung, Carl, G., The Collective Works of Carl G. Jung: Part 1, ed. by William McGuire, Princeton University Press, 2nd Edition, NJ, 1964.

11. Ibid.

12. Hegel, Georg, W., Hegel: The Essential Writings, ed. by Frederick G. Weiss,, Harper & Row, NY 1977.

13. Simpson, William, The Second Reich, Cambridge University Press, NY, 1995.

14. Fann, K.T., Wittgenstein's Conception of Philosophy, Partridge, Singapore, 2015

15. Nietzsche, Frederick, The Birth of Tragedy, Dover, NY, 1955.

16. Freud, Sigmund, Three Contributions to the Theory of Sex, Acheron Press, NY, 2012.

17. March, James, G., & Simon, Herbert, Organizations, 2nd. Edition, Blackwell Publishing, NY, 1993, pgs. 157-1189.

18. Delia, Edward, The Apocalypse, Vize, NY, 2004.

19. Ayer, A.J., Language, Truth and Logic, Dover, NY, 1952, pgs. 33-45.

20. Masters, Edgar, Lee, The Spoon River Anthology, Dover, NY, 1992, pg. 34.

Chapter 7
The Metaphysics of Knowledge

There are minute segments of phenomena of which we are aware in addition to the internal presence of our conscious self. Epistemologists often begin their analysis concerning the nature of knowledge here. This is an enormous error. Freud argued that our unconscious mind is the most significant aspect of our being. (1) It envelops both cognitive and emotional factors which are operational from early childhood onward while remaining repressed below the threshold of awareness. Other psychologists, such as Jung, have supported this essential idea.

This insight does not mean that our conscious awareness is unimportant. It does mean, however, that some rationalists, exemplified by Descartes, have been mistaken in relying on their conscious thoughts or states of mind alone in developing their arguments.

Descartes' famous dictum, *Cogito. Ergo Sum*, which has been translated as, "I think, therefore I am", is erroneous. (2) Granted there are other translations, yet A.J. Ayer for once was right when he asserted that a solitary thought is no guarantee of a systematic mind. (3) Ayer, however, an advocate of conscious linguistic analysis did not realize that there is a more potent objection to the above: namely, our existence has nothing to do with conscious interpretation. A man in a coma may not be conscious of his surroundings and his thoughts may be nil, but this fact does not negate his existence.

Our essential being is an unconscious totality or a 'lived body' in Merleau-Ponty's terms. (4) An examination of one's existence must begin in the totality of each individual's 'my being' where both consciousness and unconsciousness subsist in juxtaposition with each other.

I Am and I Am Not

Even if we were assured of our existence when we think, it would not follow that we exist in temporal sequence due to the fact that there are unavoidable lapses in our conscious thought process. I think and I do not think. Therefore, I am and I am not. This constitutes an absurdity built upon another absurdity. Yet, our organic path through temporal sequences would lead us to this conclusion.

The truth is our existence and our world are one. The world is in us and we are in the world. In Heidegger's sense, we are 'thrown into' an arbitrary world of brute facts and that world remains in us throughout life. To detach yourself from the world is to detach yourself from yourself.

The task of a great life is to 'throw back' into this arbitrary world the deed-acts of our existence. Having been 'thrown in', we have the prerogative of 'throwing back'. This constitutes our resentment over the arbitrary inequality of existence in addition to being the genesis of a singular accomplishment.

'My being' and 'my world' are one. Existence does not need to be proven.

Descartes and Darwin

Descartes was ignorant of the entire process of evolution which is usually attributed to Darwin, but was anticipated by earlier thinkers such as Anaximander and Lucretius. (5) Descartes did not reward himself of their insights or apply their ideas to his philosophy. Reason, as we know it, may not exist in lower evolutionary forms or even in primates, yet a wide range of emotion or mentality assuredly does.

Some researchers have demonstrated a limited mentality or even spiritual awareness in higher primates such as great apes. (6) Descartes, of course, was not aware of any of this as can be seen in his stated belief that a dog was a machine. (7)

The philosopher, Jacob von Uexkull, posited a systematic relationship between an organisms mental processes and the evolutionary cycle of development. (8) As eyesight differs among various species, so too does the nature of mentality. Uexkull believed that the brain develops in adaptation to the physical environment and this leads to higher or lower levels of mental capacity. Reason is not a 'logos' or finalized capacity, but a consequence of an arbitrary evolutionary sequence of events.

Descartes and Mead

In addition to physical adaptation, the capacity for reason is tied to the social environment.

There is no proposition which is self-evident-to men at all stages of life. Our limited stage of reason is not complete at birth, but rather is developmental and this development is quite slow at that.

George Herbert Mead presented a four-part model of the self, a developmental model where the self is never finalized. (9) The four aspects include the 'I' or the active self, the 'Me' or the passive self, the 'significant other' or the impact of the most important social relationships on the mind and the 'generalized other' or the general expectations of society. (10)

The details of these four aspects of the self are well-written about and will not be discussed here. What is significant, however, is that reason, which develops in connection with the emerging self, is never fully operational until late in life assuming that it is used at all. Reason is not innate, but rather develops in relation with social processes.

What is considered to be 'proper logic' has to be judged by societal standards. Kuhn is perceptive at this juncture. He believed that all cultures have paradigms of interpretation and methods of rational procedure. (11) The widespread relativity here does away with any false hope of universalism. 'Proper logic' will always be proper to some societal interest. Thus, enter the technicians of rationality.

A Processing Unit

The main reason for the failure of reason to comprehend final ends is that the brain is merely a 'processing unit' whose functioning is poorly understood. As stated previously, the brain may be governed by principles which the mind can never understand. As the brain evolves, this human 'processing unit' may gerierate an emergent logic which will reduce our current masterworks of logic to archaic absurdity. Reason is no 'logos', but is räther an empty illümination with no substance. Thus, there is no need to be puzzled by the question of mind-body interaction. There are no divergent substances at work here. All is phenomena and ideas are merely a non-substantive empty illumination.

Clear and Distinct Ideas- Descartes

Descartes, the angel of rationalism, believed that knowledge could be generated by positing what he calls 'clear and distinct' ideas. (12) He was wrong. Let us examine this contention by examining how research is conducted in the arts and sciences.

Natural scientists do not generate knowledge by positing clear and distinct ideas, but rather by controlled laboratory methods. The field of quantum mechanics was not discovered in the manner proposed by Descartes. It was the result of detailed experimentation on the nature of light and other phenomena. The same could be said for the theory of relativity.

As for social science, no sociologist or psychologist would instruct students to learn about the nature of behavior or social reality by examining clear and distinct ideas, but rather on the basis of research in which the factors of internal or external reliability or validity are controlled. What is clear and distinct in the mind apart from experimentation is often wrong.

Even in mathematics, Descartes' ideas are untenable. One plus one equals two is not clear and distinct since this is only true or a base ten system. The sum of 546 and 339 also requires rules of procedure and the designation of a base. The complex equations of algebra or calculus are neither clear nor distinct. As Godel demonstrated, there is a basic uncertainty underlying the ontology of mathematics. (13) Cantor's paradoxes concerning infinity eliminate any remaining notion of the simplicities proposed by Descartes. (14)

In addition, whatever truth there is in literature or art cannot be discerned in the manner suggested above. As Whitehead argued; what is obscure, dark or forbidden within a literary or artistic work may reveal deep structures of meaning or truth. (15) De Cherico's paintings may be shadowy and obscure, yet they are rich in symbolic significance. (16) Kafka's masterpiece. *The Trial*, presents a dark, uncertain world where absurd juxtapositions exist side by side and where nothing seems to connect with nothing, yet this work reveals profound ideas about the chaos of modern life. (17)

Actually, nothing is really clear and distinct. Descartes, of course, was referring to mathematics or intuitive philosophical certainty. He fails there and the extension of his ideas beyond this realm is an error. Even our idea of the color white as derived from an impression depends on the keenness of the human visual capacity which is variable or the intensity of light.

At various times, what we call 'whiteness' might appear differently or in different shades of 'white' with a tint of gray. Nearly all perceptions are mixed, heterogeneous and in flux. This was the basic idea conveyed by the art of the 19th Century impressionists. (18) Since our impressions are inherently tied to our ideas, our ideas must also be in flux and in juxtaposition to other ideational patterns. There are no such things as simple impressions or simple ideas.

There are no purely 'white' impressions or purely 'white' ideas. The quality of 'whiteness' never exists in pure form and in relation to ideas this is an absurdity. Within 'whiteness', there are minute shades of 'white' and infinitesimal singularities. The quest for the simple seems to be a philosophical obsession. It represents no more than a desire for an orderly world which can be built upon form simple to complex.

The Notion of Simple Objects

Philosophers are also quite fond of the notion of simple objects, Wittgenstein attempted unsuccessfully to prove their existence. (19) The truth is that all objects contain an infinity of complexes. What is called simple is so only by definition. The cell was once thought to be the basic unit of life, yet. every aspect of the cell has been revealed as the center of immense complexities.

The atom was once conceived to be the basic physical particle, but we now know that this is false. Likewise, the proton was believed to be both elementary and nearly eternal. The research of Steven Weinstein, however, has revealed that it decays and is dissolved into the myriad of the universe. (20)

In the social sciences, basic human behavior and social patters have been discerned to be incredibly complex. There are no simple answers and no basic units of analysis. If there are, it is only by arbitrary assumption.

Science as a Very Shaky Entity

Before going any further, let us note that science is a very shaký entity. It is based on a misconception: namely, that we observe an independent, objective world and can comprehend its basic ontology. The truth is quite otherwise. What we observe is phenomena upon which we impose our epistemological patterns which have themselves evolved from obscure origins.

This is best expressed in the words of Maurice Merleau-Ponty. He writes, "...we do not experience nature as an objective process or as a sort of independent complex entities, but rather what is experienced arid represented in our senses is our phenomenal field as visualized in our perception and interpreted by our embodied mind." (21)

The basic ontology of the universe or what it really is remains beyond us. The phenomenal field and axioms, assumptions or arbitrary posits are all there is. Even 'my being' is interpreted though phenomenal states of feeling or perception. What it is lies beyond the self. Yet, the attempt must be rendered which is the task of life.

Contradiction is the dialectic of life. Contradiction is my business.

The Unknown X of Destruction

Some scientists believe that they understand the basic ontology of the universe. Yet, the laws of the past do not have to be operational today or tomorrow. Nothing can be assumed anymore as the only reality which persists is 'my being'. What is coming up in the future is murderous and frightening. A world of cloning, brain transplants, artificial Intelligence and the creation of human gods. Man will attempt to transcend his limitations. But, an unknown X of destructiveness in the human brain is still operatíonal.

Freud postulated it as the 'death instinct'. (22) Hitler demonstrated it by showing that in every man there still exists the evil by which he can destroy himself. The world of Newton was beautiful and orderly, yet his ideas mean nothing in a world of arbitrary nihilism. Here and now are gone as there is no here and now. Only the basic will to survive in 'my being' is left. In the deep ocean, life lives on volcanic lave without the sun. Can man?

1. Freud, Sigmund, An Outline of Psychoanalysis, 2nd Edition, trans. by James Strachey, W.W. Norton & Co., NY & London, 1949.

2. Descartes, Rene, Meditations on the First Philosophy, trans. by Ronald A. Cress, 3rd Edition, Hackett, IN, 1993.

3. Ayer, A.J., Language, Truth and Logic, Dover, NY, 1952, pgs. 46-49.

4. Carman, Taylor, Merleau-Ponty, Routledge, London & NY, 2008.

5. Lucretius, On the Nature of the Universe, trans. by Ronald Melville, Oxford, NY, 1997.

6. Wikipedia, Gorilla.

7. Clarke, Desmond, Descartes: A Biography, Cambridge University Press, NY; 2007.

8. Uexkull, Jakob, von, A Foray into the Worlds of Animals and Humans with a Theory of Meaning, trans. by Joseph D. O'Neil, University of Minnesota press, MN, 2010.

9. Mead, George, Herbert, George Herbert Mead: On Social Psychology, trans. by Anselm Strauss, University of Chicago press, IL, 1964, pgs. 199-248.

10. Ibid.

11. Read, Rupert, Kuhn: Principles of Scientific Revolutions, Blackwell, MA, 2002, pgs. 23-96.

12. Descartes, Rene, Meditations on the First Philosophy, trans. by Donald A. Cress, 3rd Edition, Hackett, IN, 1993.

13. Nagel, Ernest & Newman, James, Godel's Proof, ed. by Douglas R. Hofstadter, New York University Press, NY 2001.

14. Dauben, Joseph, W., Georg Cantor: His Mathematics and the Philosophy of the Infinite, Princeton University Press, NJ, 1979, pgs. 219-270.

15. Whitehead, Alfred, N., Adventures of Ideas, The Free Press, NY, 1967, PGS, 241-272,

16.Merijian, Ara, H., Georgio de Chirico and the Metaphysical City, Yale University Press, Conn., 2014

17. Kafka, Franz, The Trial, Penguin Books, NY, 2016.

18. Walther, Ingo, F., ed., Impressionist Art, Taschen, Germany, 2016.

19. Wittgenstein, Ludwig, Tractatus Logico-Philosophicus, trans. C.K. Ogden, Dover, NY, 1999. Prop. 2.02-2.0211.

20. Steven Weinstein, "The Decay of the Proton", Scientific American, June 1, 1981.

21. Merleau-Ponty, Maurice, The Phenomenology of Perception, trans. Donald Landes, Routledge, NY & London, 2012. Part 2. Pg. 63.

22. Freud, Sigmund, Beyond the Pleasure Principle, ed. by James Strachey, W.W. Norton & Co., NY, 1990.

Chapter 8
The Philosophy is Me

The philosophy is me. *Le philosophies' est moi*. The first person cannot be eliminated from the philosophical equation. In any language, 'my being' is the only philosophy. This is not a solipsism, but rather a call for a redirection in philosophy. 'My being' is not only the present author's singular existence or being, but rather the 'my being' of all others. 'My being' is a combination of psychological, biological and sociological factors. Yet, it is more than that. It represents the unique in me which no one else can duplicate. No one has ever realized existence in the exact manner as I have. Thus, my vision is a creator of culture.

In relatively modern times, Heidegger was the first to call for a redirection in philosophy and for this he deserves a permanent place in the history of the discipline. (1) Being as an abstraction, however, is a misconception. This also pertains to being as it pertains to humans in the sense of a generalized Inquiry concerning what it is to be human. It is nothing. It is 'my being' or anyone's concrete existence which is his true being. The concrete is the key to the abstract. The examination of such must be the true goal of philosophy.

Objective analysis, of course, persists. Yet, we must keep in mind that concrete individuals are the foundation of this objectivity. Objective analysis is only, in Goffman's terms, a front-region activity. (2) Such a disposition should only be an intermediate stage in the analysis of 'my being'. What is termed objective is, in most cases, merely an attempt to transcend one's humanity or to pretend that an eternal force speaks through one's ephemeral existence. If our back-region was revealed, this would be less credible.

Kierkegaard was wrong. Truth is not subjectivity. Kierkegaard was discussing our relationship to the truth. (3) We are discussing the ontology of truth. If truth exists, then I am the truth. Truth relates to 'my being' and may not be relevant outside that realm. There are no Platonic ideas apart from the singular.

Science is a fake. This is not an extreme statement, but the literal truth which is ontological as embodied in 'my being'. Science has temporary utility, but little more than that. It analyzes mere juxtapositions and represents them as notations which do not envelop the ontology of the events which constitute what is real. The event is real. The eternal is enveloped in the temporal nature of 'my being'. Plurality, not unity, is the key to the temporal. Science seeks a reduction to the number one: namely, one principle, one 'logos', or one unified theory.

But, there may be billions of principles, no 'logos' and merely singular beings in a constant struggle for existence. The number one is no better than the number sixty-four except in the minds of those who desire an idealized universe. The true universe may be insane and inhuman. Frankenstein revisited!

Thus the need for a phenomenological metaphysics which analyzes the true nature of 'my being' to which all else relates including the most seemingly objective referent. The method is mostly autobiographical and the existential affirmation is paramount. All assumptions, posits, theories, rituals, beliefs or domains of interests are arbitrary extensions of my inner self. It is metaphysics and there is no way of avoiding this conclusion.

The Life of Bertrand Sovare

In an historical novella, 'The Apocalypse', a philosophical system is presented in fictional form. (3) This work was written fourteen years before the present volume. Here we attempt in a non-fictional format to exemplify the principles of interpretation underlying that earlier work as a concrete illustration of the ideas presented above.

The Apocalypse details the life of Bertrand Sovare, a former Nazi, who is detained and put on trial for alleged political crimes. His ordeal, his recollections, his prejudices and hatreds, his impotence, his dual love and hatred of Adolf Hitler and his conception of the nature of the German state constitutes the main body of this work. He also details his singular conception of existence.

The beginning of this work does not start with an abstract set of principles, but rather an existential affirmation of Sovare's 'my being'. He affirms as follows. : "What I record here is a memoir to myself. A record of my life, my experience, my world. That world is mine-it is me-and is peculiar only to me. It is not yours-it is not you- and it is not for you..

It is merely a record of events as I recall them now, no doubt colored by my specific make-up and character; yet, despite the imperfections of my memory, not to mention the physical decline of my person, I have little doubt that what now ensues corresponds to what actually happened during my captivity." (4)

Notice, he begins from the concrete center of his existence. From this center, he then presents his world-view as a récollection which is phenomenological in nature and capable of generating profound mega-abstractions interpreting the objective order in relation to his own being.

Only in this manner may his 'my being' relate to the totality and render intelligible the divine order, the social order and the natural order. In the end, this constitutes a cathedral of illumination.

This cathedral cannot be assailed. It is not based on science and is not probable. Scientific research will be translated into the strictures of phenomenology as refined in the inner life of an individual's most vital self. It is a record of a vision and that vision is eternal as it relates to 'my being'. It is a deed-act which may be modified in its thought content in the course of one's life cycle.

The Existence of the Christian God

A good example of this method can be discerned in the manner in which Bertrand Sovare speaks of the Christian God. He does not deal abstractly with objective attempts to prove or disprove the existence of the deity. He relates them to his inner being. He realizes abstract arguments unrelated to his true being have no significance and have definitely produced no consensus on this issue.

It is only as it relates to his singular existence that these disputes have importance. The argument from evil in the abstract mode does not touch him, but it is a wound as evil affects him directly. Bertrand Sovare speaks of his disbelief in God during his captivity as follows.

"Ask me for proof of God's nonexistence and I answer: Bertrand Sovare is in this state, Bertrand Sovare is living in drudgery, toil and disgrace! If there was a God, this would not be! Now, when I say there is no God, *I mean there is no principle of benevolence in relation to me.* I mean there is no abstract purpose, no moral concern, no star to guide my destiny. I mean chaos abounds, chance is prime, good seldom wins, and evil is triumphant. Above all, I mean whatever happens, happens!" (5)

135

Notice, this vision is not based on probabilities. There is no maybe or might be here. It is a deed-act which stands eternal in this temporal moment. It could be modified later by his creative self-assertion, but remains as an eternal now in the center of his existence. Others may agree or disagree, yet the ontology of truth here is in his 'my being', not yours.

The Question of Ethics

There is no greater absurdity than dealing with ethics in an objective manner. Generalized theories such as utilitarianism and deontology do not relate to 'my being'. Whether one should attempt to bring about the greatest happiness or act from a sense of formal duty must be determined by the inner self. One must start form the center of existence and move outward, not in reverse.

We are 'thrown into' this miserable world of norms and values much of which deals with ethical rules. Most of us internalize them into our superego. (6) Yet, this superego does not entirely control behavior. That is the task of the law and negative sanctions to ensure societal order.

As we develop our relatively self-determined consciousness, we attempt to 'throw-back' into the totality of being the stamp of our existence. What we 'throw-back' depends upon many factors, but one is definitely the nature of our past. An ethical system means nothing if it ignores this crucial factor.

Obviously, Adolf Hitler's ethics are despicable to most intellectuals including myself. But, Hitler was not so fortunate as myself and many others who have fine families or relative economic security. When Bertrand Sovare discusses Adolf Hitler, he speaks of his existence in society.

"The greatest of all devourers, Adolf Hitler, was merely a natural product of European society. He did not descend from the sky, but from the womb of our bifurcated race...A bestial race produced a beast. A race of angels surely would not. Hitler, after all, only reflected the excesses in human nature. His extremes were the harvest of the 'little evil' in all of us.

Ah yes, and don't demean the importance of little evil: the petty hatreds and trivial resentments, the puny struggles and minute injustices, the mild vanities or unpretentious jealousies or the countless slights or brief antagonisms that constitute so much of daily life. Are not these little evils responsible for the monstrosity we call the world? Is this not a pigmy which yields a behemoth?

Yes, little evil embodied in nameless, faceless people is now and has always been the anchor of. tyranny." (7)

Bertrand Sovare continues, "Let us consider Hitler's father, Alois. He was an abusive, violent parent. Adolf hated him- and for good reason... The beatings Adolf received were returned upon others many times over in the years that followed. Brutality breeds brutality. Consider Hitler's mother, Klara.

An overindülgent parent whom Adolf deeply loved. She was struck down by cancer at an early age... Also, consider Hitler's friends and reference groups: anti-Semitic peers, extremist military gangs or ultra-nationalist philosophers." (8)

Notice, the emphasis on concrete interactions, not abstract principles. The sort of existence Adolf Hitler lived usually does not produce a love of humanity. Man's concrete existence as embodied in his past interactions directs the type of ethical behavior any singular individual undertakes.

The point of genesis must always be concrete existence, not oracular pronouncements unconnected with that center. In the end, what we 'throw back' into the world depends upon where and when we are 'thrown in' to the human mainstream.

The Implications of this Idea

What is proposed here is not a situation ethics and does leave room for creative self-assertion. It is simply a notation that an ethical agent's past is significant in the determination of moral action. Most philosophers concentrate on the consequences of moral precepts and ignore the concrete past or present interactions which may dictate any moral choice. By understanding the great ideas, that choice may be modified by our creative self-assertion.

Very few are capable of attaining such a relative self-determination. If it is achieved, however, this represents the zenith of ethical conduct. In such a case, moral conduct is not entirely the sum of an agent's past interactions, but rather by a relatively self-imposed series of ideas to which the moral agent aspires.

This rare situation does not in any manner undermine the significance of examining those interactions and their effect on the path of moral action. The rightness or wrongness of any moral decision may, of course, be independent of such a causative examination.

How the Definition of Philosophy Affects Research

The definition of philosophy affects the manner in which philosophical problems should be approached. The abstract means nothing unless embodied in the temporal nature of 'my being'. The abstract is seen only through the concrete; the eternal is only viewed through the temporal.

The abstract is not an entity in itself devoid of concreteness or temporality. This is arrogance-an arrogance which does not touch the concrete nature of individuality. To some degree, Kant's philosophy demonstrates this characteristic. (9) Anselm was wiser in insight when he emphasized the importance of faith, in addition to reason, when considering his arguments. (10)

Abstract arguments fail as they do not touch the inner nature of 'my being' which is singular. Only a singular individual can ponder a philosophical dilemma. Philosophy relates to the concrete which is the substance of the abstract.

Yet, philosophers love abstractions and philosophy offers mega-abstractions. Kant's categorical imperative is a prime example. (11) Numerous abstractions can be found in the thought systems of Spinoza or Hegel. There is little doubt that these thinkers realize that concrete individuals, not abstract entities, render profound decisions, yet they seem to lose sight of the fact that philosophers must use language and all languages have different words, meanings and emotive associations.

Those differences should be examined in terms of their concreteness, not merely by generalizations or empty labels. Men philosophize, not machines. They live in a specific time or place and have numerous academic or non-academic associations in groups, networks and organizations.

The Task Ahead

It is now necessary to apply this conception of concrete interpretation to the fields of art, religion and ethics. All philosophical problems need concrete examination where universals acquire meaning only through the temporal or immediate, yet none necessitates such an interpretation more than the three above.

1. Heidegger, Martin, Being and Time, trans. by John Macquarrle, Harper & Row, NY, 2008

2. Goffman, Erving, The Presentation of Self In Everyday life, Anchor Books, NY, 1959.

3. Kaufman, Walter, Existentialism from Dostoevsky to Sartre, Penguin, NY, 1975.

4. Delia, Edward, The Apocalypse, Vize Publications, NY, 2004, pg. 1.

5. Ibid, pg. 9.

6. Freud, Sigmund, An Outline of Psychoanalysis, 2ND Edition, trans. By James Strachey, W.W. Norton & Co., NY & London, 1949.

7. Delia, Edward, The Apocalypse, Vize Publications, NY, 2004, pg. 18.

8. Ibid, pg. 16.

9. Kant, Immanuel, Critique of Pure Reason, Feather Trail Press, NY, 2009.

10. Anselm, Basic Writings, ed. & trans. by Thomas Williams, Hackett Publishing, IN, 2007.

11. Kant, Immanuel, Fundamental Principles of the Metaphysics of Morals, trans. Thomas K. Abbott, CreateSpace Independent Publishing Platform, 2016.

Chapter 9
Art, Religion and Ethics

Philosophy of Art

The discipline of aesthetics explores the meaning and significance of art, music and dance. In regard to art, there is no general definition of the term since art is too complex a phenomenon for any simple formula or solution to suffice.

Art is a human technology- a way of improving the value or enjoyment of life. It is a projection of the inner being of every singular artist. If there is no consensus concerning its meaning, this is due to the fact that every individual's 'my being' differs from every other.

It has been asserted in an abstract, superficial manner that the purpose of art is to evoke an appreciation of beauty. Yet, it is doubtful whether anyone, after due consideration, would render so simple an abstraction. Beauty is in itself hard to define and can be quite subjective in its application. Of course, there have been attempts to list the objective elements constituting beauty - line, balance, color coordination or design - yet, the subjective element cannot be eliminated. (1) That subjective element radiates from every individual's 'my being'. It could even be argued that what is considered objective stems from every singular artist's inner nature.

There might have been a consensus that the paintings of Rembrandt or Claude evoked beauty, but it would be far from certain that the paintings of Jackson Pollack would. (2) The latter's paintings to appeal to something far from beauty and perhaps from sanity itself. (3).

Sometimes a painting is referred to as beautiful, yet this was not the artist's intention or even the main reason for the painting's greatness. Consider Caravaggio's, *A Boy Bitten by a Lizard*. (4) Some may call this painting beautiful. But, is it? It may be painted adroitly, yet it presents a boy in pain just after being bitten by a cold-blooded animal. How can the calamity of pain be considered beautiful? This seems absurd. In truth, the greatness of the painting lies elsewhere: namely, in its emphasis on the primacy of the moment. Caravaggio is suggesting that the 'right now' should be the purpose of art, not the eternal essence.

In a famous definition, Santayana defined beauty as 'objectified pleasure'. (5) Yet, this suggestion put forward by this profound mind is not as helpful as it initially might seem. The objective does not speak through Santayana and he would be the first to agree with that statement. As with all definitions, this formulation is a projection of his inner being in intersection with his phenomenological experience.

Beyond this, pleasure itself envelops several diverse human emotions or rational attitudes and there is little consensus as to its essence. On rare occasions, it simply refers to reinforcement or repetition. If an animal repeats a certain behavior associated with enjoyment, that behavior is said to be pleasurable. Behaviorists talk of a 'pleasure center' in animals to explain their conditioning. Yet, on what rational grounds do we have a right to call that a 'pleasure center due to the dull fact of reinforcement? On physiological grounds, one could state that certain animal behaviors are conductive to enhancing metabolism or other life processes and in that manner justify this assumption. Yet, even that could be disputed since certain behaviors enhancing life processes could be painfül.

Many believe that art is an imitation of nature. One visit to any good art museum might dispute this naïve contention. Consider Rembrandt's, *Portrait of Aechje Claesdr*, which is in the National Gallery in London. (6) Clearly, this is a masterful, naturalistic depiction of an eighty-three-year-old woman. But, Turner's painting, *Dido Building Carthage*, or DeChiraco's. *The Great Metaphysician*, speak rather of the world of the imagination. (7) Rousseau's paintings reveal the world of fantasy. (8) Other art works may have a religious meaning and so on.

Experts in meta-aesthetics have debated what is called the 'intentional fallacy' and the 'affective fallacy'. (9) The former concerns whether the artist's intention should be the basis of criticism while the latter deals with whether the audience's reaction to a painting should comprise that basis. These. debates come and go endlessly to little purpose.

The truth is that the meaning of art is multifaceted. There is no magic bullet that expresses its value in a single formula. This is not only true of painting, but also of other forms of art. Great art might express beauty, but also reveal a new technique, or a novel idea on how to express perspective or even the bold use of an invented pigment. Since man is an evolving animal, both physically and socially, that evolution will result in novel ideas which will endlessly be expressed in art.

Metaphysically, art is an expression of human value- a statement that there must be more to life than a mere animal existence. Every man must reach within himself to discover what is unique in his being. An artist externalizes that uniqueness.

It must also be realized, however, that these conscious motivational intentions of the artist stem from a non-motivational factor: namely, the attempt to touch the base of the Being-itself by transcending the grammatical structure of language and specifically the 'iron chain' of subject-object dualism. Art negates the idea that the limits of our language are the limits of our world. In art, we are free of the tyranny of language. Rene Magritte's paintings, *Oasis* and he *Empire of Light* free us from conventional spatial and temporal proportionality in addition to the rules or customs connected with it. In the latter painting, the light of reason becomes the main source of confusion.

Philosophy of Music

Music is auditory art and the same problems listed above relate to discovering its essence. Music has profound effects on us both psychologically and in terms of socio-historical experience. The most profound theory of music is Schopenhauer's; the most stimulating is Steven Pinker's. (10)

The latter Harvard authority labels music as 'auditory cheesecake' a spandrel- an unnecessary capacity developed in evolutionary sequence in relation to more necessary genes essential for survival. (11) This stimulating idea suggests that this human capacity was neither intentional nor necessary and is the by-product of more mundane mechanisms. So much for the thought that human life is an expression of natural, ideal intentions in an orderly universe.

Schopenhauer's theory of music must be understood in relation to his metaphysics. (12) To his mind, music is a copy of the Will in nature- a non-temporal, non-spatial inner core of reality. This is why the effect of music is more powerful than the other arts. They speak only of shadows while music speaks for the thing itself- the inner core of being.

Both these conceptions are insightful, yet have brought no consensus. The reason is that the meaning of music stems from the 'my being' of every individual and collectively from the civilization or nation which, after all, is a collection of its individual citizens. Music enhances romance, ceremony, war, revolution and dance. It can enhance, nationalism as evidenced by the French National Anthem, *La Marseillaise*. It can enable a noble resistance to invasion as seen in the *Leningrad Symphony* in 1941-42. (13) It can also facilitate leisure, sexuality, spiritual transcendence and utopian desires.

Since dance is one of the most important forms of non-verbal communication, the relationship between dance and music when properly explored can reveal deep structures of meaning concerning the human condition. This is particularly true since most non-verbal behavior is innate. (14) In the end, in a non-verbal, almost transcendent manner, music touches the inner nature of our being or uniqueness.

Philosophy and Religion

Religion is a my being experience. Abstract arguments, as stated previously, do not relate or touch my inner essence. I must speak in the first person here. Standard texts can be read concerning the so-called proofs for and against the existence of god. They all fail and for good reason. No one comes to god through the intellect.

(As an existential affirmation, it seems to the present author that in religion man is grasping for something he knows not in order to attain something radically different from the present world of murder and greed. He cannot believe that this benighted world is all there is to existence. Man lives by hope and this is the ultimate one. A mighty force in the sky, a spirit of decency, who will deliver us from evil.

Illusions do not fit well in a world of realities. Men go to church and pray and pray and often those prayers go unanswered. Christ's appearance on earth did not lead to a 'golden kingdom', but rather to a continuation of the kingdoms of greed and murder right up to the present time. Most of mankind has never heard of Jesus Christ. At present, two-thirds of the world's population either worships other deities or has no religion at all. Also, some religions do not have a well-developed conception of god.

The way I view Christ, he was a people lover. He took joy in mere existence. He probably was impressed by the strangeness that anything should exist at all. He loved every feature of every person or beast or vegetation. He believed that every imperfection would be corrected in some future kingdom of God. His talk of hell was merely a lapse of annoyance, not to be taken seriously.

His inner decency mandated a strict code of ethics which he preached with idealism. Did this spark of decency derive from God? It cannot be denied, yet it cannot be affirmed. Scripture is not history. Will he come back to judge both the living and the dead? I dare not say.

As to my position as stated previously in a fictional format, I have doubts concerning God's existence since there is no principle of benevolence in relation to me. I see little purpose to existence and the near universality of injustice everywhere in a brutal universe. I see the triumph of evil and the fall of decency. Every day that passes is a day without God. Yet, at other times, I think differently and hope that there is an ultimate reason for existence beyond the biological imperative. It is strange that anything should exist at all. Pure logic could lead me to different conclusions, yet logic is not the key to life.)

This first-person affirmation is a psychological-logical or existential posit, not to be confused with formal arguments which prove nothing. The ontological argument was justly referred to by Schopenhauer as a 'charming joke'. A being than which nothing greater can be conceived is nonsense. What is meant by the phrase 'nothing greater' could be defined and redefined in an endless series of disputes. There is no reason to believe that any mental conception has any reality outside the mind in terms of pure logic alone. Existence, as Kant argued, is not a predicate. (15)

The first cause argument also fails miserably. It seems that the universe should have a first cause, yet there is no necessity here. It is possible that there is no first cause, but only an endless regression of causes with no origin. Even if there is a first cause, it might be some feature of the universe such as electro-magnetism or atomic structure. The concept of causation itself has been questioned. (16) Moreover, even if this argument demonstrated the existence of god, it would not necessarily be the Christian God. Other so-called proofs of God's existence suffer a similar fate.

As stated, there is no desire here to analyze all the formal arguments for the reality of the deity. But, it is too tempting not to comment on the design argument which Christians often assert.

I have little doubt that Bertrand Russell was correct when he asserted that there is no greater absurdity than the belief that this world and all the things in it could be designed by an all-good, all-powerful God. (17) This is a world where larger animals devour smaller ones, disasters prevail, injustice is omnipresent and human dreams often crumble within the debris. A benevolent all-powerful creator would never sustain such a world of inferiority.

Now, while God's existence cannot be proven by objective argumentation, the opposite is also true.

Philosophical arguments cannot disprove the existence of God. The argument from evil raises doubts, yet it is often asserted that the world is better with evil in it- that it gives man a chance to demonstrate his moral fiber. (18) Other justifications of evil are often given and no consensus is ever reached on either side. The theory of

147

evolution, of course, is a grand argument against the Christian account of creation. But, creationists deny its veracity pointing to what they regard as alternative evidence. (19)

They believe man was created by God 'ex nihilo' or out of nothing. Yet, they seem not to realize what this concept of nothingness implies. By their own definition, God is an absolute, being-in-itself. As such, God is devoid of nothingness. In metaphysics, nothing is not empty space or physical space which is a continuous field of activity. Nothing is not in space or in time, but rather a pure negation. How could the ground of being be related to non-being? Heidegger foresaw this dilemma. (20)

(Several comments are in order here. First, this view that the world is better with evil in it is not credible unless you believe that cancer hospitals and assassinations enhance the perfection of life.

Second, the theory of evolution is backed by an enormous body of evidence derived from the scientific method which is a method whose veracity has been questioned in this treatise. Yet, we must use the tools we have and rely on a method whose veracity is greatly in question.

There may, be a contradiction here, but the idea of contradiction is merely a unit assumption in the Western conventional wisdom prevalent within scientific circles. As philosophers, we may accept numerous contradictions within our world-view and regard them as an illumination or a conduit enhancing the great cathedral. Third, our fondness for phenomenology is not threatened by examining scientific research as that body of insights may later be reinterpreted by phenomenologists.)

Philosophers with few exceptions do not like to rely upon authority. Yet, they seem willing to rely upon the conclusions of an impersonal, rational capacity which supposedly belongs to all and, therefore, to no one in particular. This impersonal, objective approach is useless when reaching for God, Only the singular individual in his total concreteness may hope to touch the base of holiness. It is written that the pure of heart will see God. Perhaps philosophers should do less thinking in objective terms and look profoundly or subjectively within their inner being. This is not a relativism as every singular argument concerning God is not equal to every other. Each must be evaluated individually and some may be superior just as ancient Greek civilization was superior to others during that period. All must be consulted, yet some may be more profound.

A Word About Immortality

Philosophers have spent much time analyzing the disparate ideas of immortality. Many civilizations have exhibited these ideas. Here we will examine the Christian version. In general, Christianity is an irrational system. It must be accepted on authority and faith since it makes little sense rationally. Why did God create a weak race prone to sin? Why did he have to sacrifice his only begotten son for the redemption of mankind? Answers could be provided here, yet none has been widely accepted.

The Christian belief in immortality is, however, the most irrational. The belief in immortality is independent of the belief in God. You may believe in God and deny immortality and vice versa. Christians have a tendency to connect the two. The Christian belief posits the resurrection of the body, not the body used on earth, but a divinely created body. This idea leads to a series of absurdities that even the most dogmatic believer cannot ignore. This divinely created body of the Last Judgement is supposed to be perfect or devoid of disease.

This raises the question as to why God did not render this ideal body to man here on earth. Of course, Christians will respond that the deity did create man perfectly before the imperfection of original sin. This raises the additional question as to why God punishes all mankind over hundreds of generations for this one primitive deviance. Once again, these endless questions have no final answer. Philosophers should avoid these dead ends, but this is not easy since the absurdities of Christianity mandate examination. As for this divinely created body, does it resemble the original one? We often recognize people on the basis of how they look. If it doesn't, how could this be the same person? If it does, at what age does it resemble the person?

At ten, thirty-one or seventy-seven? Further, do they wear clothes? If they don't, it might be humiliating to run into your great-aunt ant the Last Judgement. If they do, where would they procure their clothes? Paul Edwards once commented that Christians seem to believe that there is a celestial retail store in the sky.

There are more profound questions here. This spiritual body is supposed to be perfect, unlike the earthly body. But, what exactly is a spiritually perfect body? By definition, the human body is an organic entity mostly dependent upon carbon bonding for a finite duration and with definite limitations. A body is a 'lived body'. A dead body is a corpse. There is no meaning to personal identity before birth or after death.

Man is enveloped within finiteness. Human activities are directly connected with bodily functions and have no meaning apart from them. The social world man learns about itself has a limited duration. Finiteness is the key to man's existence. We are born and then we die.

As for heaven and hell, this seems to be divine despotism. Why should man's behavior mandate an eternal reward or condemnation? An eternal sanction seems unjust! Every Christian wants to go to heaven, yet no one seems to know what you do there. An infinite servitude to an eternal order would not be paradise. Rather, it would be an eternal boredom without aspiration, struggle or achievement. In short, the least desired end for those who live in the ideal, As for hell, this seems to be a place of torture as it would be conceived by Ivan the Terrible. Hell is the most obnoxious, despicable idea ever conceived by the perverted mind of man. It is unthinkable to conceive of a just God burning helpless humans!

One more note especially for those who bow to the alter of science. Christian claims above are contradicted by the findings of modern bio-physics. Scientists claim that life is a late development in the history of the universe. There was no life in the universe for billions of years. The earth has an enormous record of extinctions. It is possible that man could be one of them. No extinct creature has ever reappeared.

The truth is that the eternity of life is an absurdity. Men are born and die. Accept this and you will sleep easier. Immortality is a futile dream of idle minds who cannot accept the realities of existence. That reality is that finiteness is the key to life.

(As an existential affirmation, this is what the higher thought processes dictate. Yet, in my total concreteness, I often negate the eye of reason and hope that the beliefs of Christianity could be true. It is said that Santayana was an atheist who believed that Mary was God's mother. I am an agnostic who believes in the infinite riches of Christ.)

Philosophy and Ethics

The presuppositions underlying ethics are that man possess the freedom to choose between rationally selected alternatives and that the ethical alternative is the ultimate criterion for enlightened action. Both these assumptions are false. As discussed previously, most human behavior and all lower organic functions are determined by physical-chemical or social causes. The only freedom man can achieve derives from the contemplation of ideals or mega-abstractions which circumvent in their infinite combinations causative or functional mandates. An ideal or mega-abstraction is not a thing, like Saint Patrick's Cathedral, subject to material impact or functional manipulation. It is a deed-act, a leap to freedom. A titan of all titans. Very few can attain this leap to freedom, yet when it is achieved the world is illuminated. Only the titans can act ethically in terms their own creative self-awareness though they have no right to assume that others should follow their dictates. Even the titans may be fallible.

The vast amount of the human race must rely upon social mores as the basis of their ethical behavior. These mores are internalized during socialization and exercise an external constraint upon ethical behavior. The first mandate of any society is to ensure public safety and mores are the first line of defense in that they are backed up by sanctions. Otherwise, every singular individual would do whatever he pleases and the result would be chaos. Thinkers may comment upon these mores, but they can never replace or undermine them on a societal basis. No one can invent a comprehensive ethical system for all mankind. It would be similar to firing a bullet at a mountain. The mountain would remain intact.

This, of course, does not mean that the work of the titans of ethical philosophy are in vain. They are attempting to invent the ideal morality or identify the basis of moral obligation or the functions of ethical language. It does mean that the mores formed over centuries and internalized through socialization lie at the root of our moral code, ethical imperatives or societal functioning.

Why should I be moral? Some philosophers believe that this is a meaningless question since the moral reason is the ultimate reason for enlightened action. But, they are wrong. The founder of existentialism demonstrated this in a brilliant analysis of Abraham's actions while attempting to kill his son upon the orders of God. Clearly killing his son violated the commandment prohibiting murder, yet Abraham decided to kill his progeny due to his conviction that obeying God's commands was more important than any ethical precept. Theology transcended ethics. Of course, God stopped the murder. In fact, the law-whether civil or divine-transcends ethics. The law prevents deviance by its presence. (21)

The "my being' of every individual must determine his response to ethics and that individual must be prepared to accept the consequences of his response. This is not a situation ethics since some ethical actions are superior. Yet, attempts at a universal ethics must fail since every human being is a specific case. The particulars must be examined including past behavior, not just future consequences. Life is too complex for a one-dimensional ethical system which negates the past as instrumentalism does despite the fact that this system is complex in many other ways.

One more thing. Since Hume, it has been said that you can't derive an 'ought' from an 'is'. Yet, in the above sense, mores are social facts and do represent an 'is' and the factual basis of 'oughtness'. Spinoza's ideas also exhibit this characteristic. To his mind, all human behavior is determined, yet the realization of this determination through adequate ideas represents the highest ethical ideal. 'Thus, an 'ought' is derived from an 'is' in his ethical system. In truth, all ethical action exhibits 'factual oughtness'.

Moreover, William Frankena has rendered a classic statement challenging this Humean assumption. (22)

1. Hogarth, William, The Analysis of Beauty, ed. by Ronald Paulson, Dover Publications, Mineola, NY, 2015.

2. Rembrandt, Jacob Trip, 1661, National Gallery in London..

3. Neifeh, Steven & Smith, Gregory, Jackson Pollack: An American Saga, Woodward/White Inc., 3rd ed., NY, 2014.

4. Caravaggio, Boy Bitten by a Lizard, 1594-96, National Gallery in London.

5. Santayana, George, A Sense of Beauty: Being the Outline of Aesthetic Theory, Dover, Mineola, NY, 1955.

6. Rembrandt, Portrait of Aechje Claesdr, 1634, National Gallery I London.

7. Georgio de Chiraco, The Great Metaphysician, Museum of Modern Art, NY; J.M.W. Turner, Dido Building Carthage, 1815, National Gallery in London.

8. Henri Rousseau, The Dream, 1910. Museum of Modern Art, NY.

9. Leitch, Vincent, ed. The Norton Anthology of Theory and Criticism, W.W. Norton & Co. 2001.

10. Schopenhauer, Arthur, The World as Will and Representation, E.F.J. Payne, trans, Dover, Mineola, NY, 1969, pgs. 167-268.

11. Pinker, Steven, How the Mind Works, W.W. Norton & Co. 1998.

12. Schopenhauer, Arthur, The World as Will and Representation, E.FJ. Payne, trans, Dover, Mineola, NY, 1969, pgs. 269-412.

13. Shostakovich, Dmitri, Symphony No. 7 in C Major, (Leningrad), 1939-1942.

14. The Journal of Personality and Social Psychology, Vol. 96, No. 1, January 2009.

15. Kant, Immanuel, Critique of Pure Reason, trans. by Werner S. Plumar, Hackett Classics, IN, pg. 578-585.

16. Coventry, Angela, Hume's Theory of Causation: A Quasi-Realist Interpretation, Continium International Publishing Group, NY 2006, pgs. 89-104.

17. Russell, Bertrand, Why I Am Not a Christian, Touchstone, Simon & Schuster, NY, 1997.

18. Mackie, J.L., Evil and Omnipotence, Mind, 64 (254), April, 1955, pgs. 200-212.

19. Collins, Francis, S., The Language of God, NY, The Free Press, 2006.

20. Heidegger, Martin, Being and Time, Harper & Row, NY, 2005.

21. Kierkegaard, Soren, Fear and Trembling, trans.by Alastair Hannay, Penguin, NY, 1995.

22. Frankena, William, K., Ethics, 2nd Edition, Prentice-Hall, NJ, 1973.

Postscript: Conclusions and Recommendations

The ideas expressed in this book are a product of creative self-assertion after a long period of thinking and philosophical research. While some conclusions may seem extreme, they are not hasty and are supported by much of the Western philosophical tradition. That tradition was in large part influenced by the pre-Socratics in both metaphysics and moral philosophy. 'My being' was shaped by that tradition. My purpose here is not to summarize the entire book, but rather to stress several specific conclusions or recommendations.

First, being is embodied in man's finiteness. 'My being' is existential-it is a deed-act derived from a concrete self. There is no such thing as being-in-itself or 'human being' as a generic notion or broad abstraction. 'My being' is quasi-isolated, finite, singular- indeed, autobiographical and enveloped within broad bifurcations. It is quasi-isolated because I am in the world and the world is in me. Thus, all delineations of 'my being' are semi-isolated, mosaic ones. Delineations by others-that is, other minds-are 'wounds' within the self which are often cited as mere biography. Yet, autobiography is the key. The key to the 'map', yet not the true self.

Second, the conception of the metaphysics of 'my being' is derived from an analysis of the meaning of philosophy itself as seen in the previous pages. Thus, the meaning of philosophy determines the methodology of philosophy.

Third, the nature of reason must be reexamined using not only philosophical analysis, but also the findings of the specialized sciences. Philosophical analysis must be phenomenological. Reason is not an entity in itself, a light of illumination or a key to history, but the mere by-product of a 'processing unit' known as the human brain. The ultimate question of naturalized epistemology must be the following: namely, what exactly is logic and how does it relate to any organic entity? (1) This query is not new as Hobbes' philosophy renders ideas to be a by-product of sensation.

Fourth, philosophical research must include existential affirmations which reveal the author's inner being. Objective analysis is a front-region persona which negates the individual's concreteness. It has much utility, but also hides a great truth: namely, that the concrete is the truth. Montaigne and Schopenhauer's first-person essays are excellent in this regard. (2) The mode of soliloquy in Shakespeare should exemplify the ideal mode. (3)

Fifth, the other sources of knowledge such as authority, faith, intuition, mysticism and common sense must be more widely respected in philosophy. The underworld of logic is based upon these other sources and philosophers have no right to disrespect them. Moreover, human cognition often develops in connection with faith, intuition, common sense and authority. Spinoza regarded intuition as the primary level of knowledge and Reid extolled the value of common sense. There is more sense in common sense than most philosophers believe.

Sixth, philosophical study must include more fiction including novels, plays, short stories and poetry. Quality music and art should also be referenced. This idea has antecedents in the work of Goethe, Voltaire and the 20th Century existentialists. (4) I would also include quality movies during the early part of that century.

Seventh, philosophers should follow a phenomenological method with more emphasis on autobiography in order to achieve a cathedral of illumination. This will stand as a record of a vision.

A vision which is eternal as expressed through the temporal and avoids the dull possibilities of objective analysis. A vision which reveals 'my being' though not, in Heidegger's terms, any universal essence of Being. (5) The basic ideas of the phenomenological method, of course, were derived from Husserl. (6)

Eight, philosophical research must reject any notion of general definitions. Thinkers from Whorf to Derrida have laid the foundations of this recommendation. (7)

Ninth, ethical, aesthetic and religious notions must be interpreted in terms of the concrete. What is beautiful, what is holy or what is moral is only given flesh in the singular, concrete encounter. Many sages from Buber to Lyotard have stressed this idea. (8) Hegel himself posited the concrete universal.

Tenth, philosophers should have more respect for the embodiment thesis: namely, that most aspects of cognition are shaped not only be the brain, but also by other features of the body. This would include the perceptual system, the motor system and other organ functions. (9) Man is a 'lived body' and most aspects of existence must be understood through that prism.

Eleventh, freedom is not a given, but rather an achievement. Most lower bodily functioning is determined by physical-chemical or social factors, yet during the highest levels of cognitive thought as per mega-abstractions, a 'leap to freedom' is achieved. This achievement is equivalent to becoming a titan.

Finally, there are no certainties, but only probabilities. Of course, the notion of probability implies a limited conception of order. But, that order is ephemeral and in process. Thus, all things are possible and anything can occur. Some things are more likely than others, that's all.

Now, even within myself, these beliefs are not final. They only relate to 'my being'. They are a product of my intentionality and also my non-intentionality as per states of consciousness devoid of an object. Herein is a major disagreement with Husserl. In the end, I sometimes wonder whether mere survival is all that counts. I have reached above to touch the hand of God without affect. At times, I glance below the level of human interest.

The murderous head of a fly knows of no highest good, nor logic, nor science. Yet, the existence of his species is secure and might transcend ours in time. Now, Pascal would suggest that man is greater in that his mind embraces the universe. Of course, Pascal did realize the full range of bestiality in human nature, as Shakespeare did. The latter wrote that man often has 'bad dreams'. (10) As for the fly, as he bites into Pascal's flesh, he would answer, if he could, in Pascal's native tongue. **"Embrasse-moi!"** Likewise, I say to my critics, **"Embrasse-moi!"**

1. Quine, W.V.O., Naturalized Epistemology, Perceptual Knowledgeand Ontology, ed. by Leon Decock & Lieven Horsten, Rodopi Publishing, 2016.

2. Montaignė, Michel, de, Montaigne: The Complete Essays, trans. by M.A. Screech, Penguin, NY, 1993.

3. Shakespeare, William, Hamlet, ed.by Barbara A. Mowat & Paul Werstine, Simon & Schuster, NY, 2012.

4. Kaufman, Walter, Existentialism from Dostoevsky to Sartre, Penguin, NY, 1975.

5. Heidegger, Martin, Being and Time, trans, by John Macquarrie, Harper & Row, NY, 2008.

6. Husserl, Edmund, Ideas: General Introduction to Pure Phenomenology, trans. by-W. R. Boyce Gibson, Routledge Classics, NY, 2004.

7. Whorf, Benjamin, Language, Thought and Reality, ed. by John B. Carroll, Selected Writings by Benjamin Whorf, M.I.T. Press, 1956.

8. Lyotard, Jean-Francols, The Post Modern Condition: A Report on Knowledge, trans. by Geoff Bennington & Brian Massumi, University of Minnesota Press, MN, 1989.

9. Varela, Francisco, Thompson, Evan, & Rosch, Eleanor, The Embodied Mind: Cognitive Science and Human Experience, Cambridge, MA, M.I.T. Press, 1991.

10. Shakespeare, Willlam, Hamlet, eds. Barbara A. Mowat & Paul Werting, Simon & Schuster, 1992. Act 2, Scene 2.

PART THREE

Appendix 1 - Technical Remarks

The following detailed technical remarks are reserved for this appendix as a consequence of my firm belief that a philosopher should attempt to write for the enlightenment of all humanity and not only for philosophical specialists. Thus, the text is presented in a manner consistent with the mentality of the layman in his relatively self-determined desire to broaden his intellectual vision. The following technical remarks are meant for those who require more detail due to their academic training.

Chapter 1

1. "The foundation of philosophy requires considerable cultural development as its blueprint which when complete will allow a systematic index of the wealth of knowledge to be built upon it."

Commentary: I am absolutely convinced that philosophy could never have been the first cause of mental development, but rather must have rested upon a prior cultural liberation in the form of of ideas on how to live including, but not exclusive of, dance, folkways, music or other symbolic communications. However, this foundation is only its blueprint and not its construction which is seen in the history of philosophy. As philosophy develops in its unfolding, it merely provides an index and not the complete detail of what must be built upon this foundation. Foundationalism, as in Descartes, has never been universally justified and there is no claim here that the above referred to wealth of knowledge will ever or can ever be built.

2. "Now, it is often easier to recognize what is not than to perceive what is."

Commentary: I am not and will never be a slave to prior terminology. I realize that perception is usually reserved for sensory observation while conception is reserved for mental awareness. This is a false distinction. The two are interrelated and cannot be distinguished. My senses and cognition operate together to produce judgements which is consistent with Kant's view.

Also, what is and what is not are interrelated. They are not separate or non-identical. As Hegel would affirm, being and non-being are two points on a continuum which will lead to a synthesis. What is not reveals to us what is. I know myself in part from what I am not. How do I know that I am a teacher? Well, because I have students. Student and teacher exist not apart, but in relation. In Hegel's terms, how do I know that I am a master? Obviously, because I have a servant. No servant, no master. Hence, by recognizing what philosophy is not, I uncover the direction toward which the truth may be found.

3. "Science is one thing, philosophy is another."

Commentary: I recognize that science and philosophy were regarded as almost identical until the end of the 19th Century or that some of the greatest scientists have been philosophers as in the case of Leibniz. I also realize that the two fields have deeply influenced each other. What I wish to indicate here is that the two disciplines are distinct in regard to the criteria of quantification. Now, while all ideas are in process, I can visualize no unified synthesis in terms of a new discipline, but only the merging of ideas from one to the other. That is, science affecting philosophy and philosophy influencing science. Hence, we have Leibniz reasoning against the Newtonian system in regard to the quantitative language of

163

advanced mathematics. What happens if matter is traduced in motion? What is left? In elementary terms, energy! Thus, the notion of the monad. The rest is history.

4. "Whitehead keenly wrote that nearly all philosophy is a series of footnotes to Plato."

Commentary: I wish to note that this could be due to the fact that Plato wrote the first systematic philosophy since the detailed writings of the pre-Socratics have been lost to humanity. Arthur Holmes, a delightful Englishman and profound historian of philosophy, used to say that in the last two hundred years most of philosophy has been a series of footnotes to Hegel. He might be correct. Hegel has influenced German idealism, existentialism, phenomenology, philosophy of language, Marxism and numerous other major theoretical developments. Probably, Hegel should be placed fifth on the list of the most influential thinkers.

Chapter 2

5. "By reduction, the ultimate 'truths' of reflection may stem from our genes, not our minds."

Commentary: The idea of a biological 'a priori' might give support to Plato's belief that the attainment of truth is a recollection of ideas derived from a previous existence. This would mean that they are innate or inborn. In a 20th Century sense, that would be congruent with the notion of archetypes being transmitted by genes from one generation to the next.

6. 'We understand little of the cosmos and have a sense of awe or wonder at its seeming majesty."

Commentary: In Aristotle's cosmos, all beings except god are 'governed' by a sense of wonder in regard to the notion of final cause. This is an inner theology of being. A universe 'moved' by wonder due to the gap between potentiality and actuality which exists in all beings except god whose nature constitutes pure actuality.

7. "It should be noted that Plato believed that the love of wisdom or truth is evident only in philosopher-kings which gives them the right to govern."

Commentary: This should be interpreted as meaning that the philosopher-kings exhibit wisdom after finishing the training period Plato advocates as a prerequisite for governance. In a historical sense, the present author disagrees. If there is anything that has been a plague to the world, it is the governance by intellectuals. Robespierre and Lenin were intellectuals. As I have written previously, intellectuals love books, not people. There are exceptions, yet this basic insight remains intact. As Plato, most intellectuals cherish ideas more than individuals and theories more than humanity.

8. "The truth may be hidden in the recesses of our unconscious."

Commentary: This is an additional reason to examine the most intimate details of a philosopher's life. In Hobbes' case and by his own admission, the element of fear becomes vital in understanding the direction of his thinking. He lived through the barbarous English Civil War and could see what human nature is capable of devoid of institutional control. His desire to establish the legitimacy of the state is the key, not the pure, value-free pursuit of truth. He desired peace and harmony, above all.

9. "All ideas may change in time."

Commentary: This, of course, is Hegel's basic insight. There is no such thing as a static category. All concepts evolve and take on novel symbolic meanings. They may move in the direction of thesis, antithesis, synthesis or, in an existentialist sense, in the direction of thesis, antithesis with no synthesis. The latter case would pertain to thinking about God. There is no necessary reason why a synthesis should occur. It often does, yet at times does not. Here we reach the limit of language and cognitive understanding. Hence, the door is opened to faith and authority.

10. "The truth is that they are, that is, Platonic ideals, the arbitrary constructs of the human mentality."

Commentary: Great minds often commit great flaws. This is Plato's grand mistake: namely, that there are universals which subsist independently of the mind and can be ascertained in an 'a priori' manner. Augustine combined this doctrine with Christion belief to portray Christ as a divine 'logos'. Even Whitehead utilized this belief in his conception of the primordial nature of god. God embodies eternal possibilities which he gives to the world to produce a satisfaction. The purpose of Plato's doctrine is to provide an ordered harmony to the cosmos. Yet, there is no 'a priori' reason why we should believe in this conception of eternal divine essences. The truth is that the universe may have only a temporary, fragmented order due to the mutual adjustment of phenomena. If one speaks of probabilities, this presupposes such a belief in ephemeral patterns of order, yet in no manner does this imply any belief in a 'logos' in either Stoic or Christian form. As Hume suggested, there couldn't be a universe unless certain aspects of reality were adjusted to certain others. However, this consideration in no manner implies that this fragmented order was imposed by a divine mind or by an inherent 'telos' in the natural order.

11. "In a contrary domain, A would not equal A."

Commentary: This reminds me of Wittgenstein's famous example. He asserted, "Green is green." This is not as simple as you might think. The first green might refer to Mr. Green and the second to his envy. Of course, Aristotle meant that A could not equal not A at the same time and in the same respect. Yet, this situation does not and can never exist. Time is continuous and directional. Every second consists of multiple microseconds. Also, nothing is exactly alike any other in the same respect. Aristotle dislikes Plato's doctrine of independently subsisting essences devoid of particulars. But, in his logic, he creates an ideal form that never exists in any particular. This is Aristotle's contradiction. Hegel would respond that contradiction is the law of reality. We all exhibit contradictions as does the historical process.

12. "...there is no reason in the first place to expect the future to resemble the past."

Commentary: The only reason why we expect the future to resemble the past is that the mind is not, as the Stoics and John Locke believed, a 'tabula rasa' or blank tablet. The mind does have, in Aristotle's terms, potentiality and one of those potentials seems to be a tendency to inquire about the origin of circumstances which we interpret according to the principles of reason. We notice certain aspects of reality or phenomena are conjoined to certain others in regularity and try to draw universal conclusions. The problem is that the actual ontological functioning of the universe is independent of any epistemological presuppositions posited by our limited intellect.

13. "Total freedom devoid of authority would lead us into a hell where there is no reason."

Commentary: It is absurd to hope for total freedom or the type of freedom advocated during the Enlightenment. Look inward and imagine what a disaster you would create if you had total freedom to do whatever you wanted. Freedom is useful only in a limited sense in relation to societal control. This was Emile Durkheim's basic concern: namely, the relation of freedom and authority. Absolute power corrupts absolutely as human nature devoid of social control is evil in the sense of having a limited or, for that matter, no regard for the rights of others. Consider the breakdown of societal order during the Peloponnesian War or during the last days of the Third Reich and you can see what human nature is devoid of sane authority. Hitler had the power of life and death over every German and the results are well documented.

Jean-Paul Sartre's philosophy posits a belief in total freedom for the individual. He does not believe in a permanent self as we recreate the self every time we act. The self is enveloped in qualities, states and actions. Kant's idea of a transcendental self is rejected. This philosophy pushes to the absolute limit the belief in total freedom. Yet, freedom for what and to what purpose? We exist in a dialectical relationship to society and to others.

The concept of 'my being' envelops a 'world' of interest. Apart from that world, I am nothing. Sartre seems to realize this when he stresses that we know ourselves through what we are not. How do I know that I am a master? Well, due to the fact that I have a servant! Yet, he doesn't realize how the consequence of this admission undermines the veracity of his belief in total freedom. If I am born in a social web, that web of statuses and roles creates obligations which limit my freedom. My identity is defined in that network of social relations. Moreover, if there is no permanent self, how can I explain my enduring psychological and behavioral regularities? Now, the self does change, but there must be some enduring nucleus of self which constitutes 'my being' even during the process of becoming.

Another problem with Sartre's philosophy is that total freedom implies that there is no limit to possibilities. If I'm totally free, all possibilities are available to me. All those possibilities would overwhelm the average mind. One of the functions of the social order is to limit the range of possibilities available to the individual. Whitehead realized that there must be a limit to possibilities and this is one of the functions of god.

A universe of total possibilities is a universe of madness. One more thing. The essential function of the state can be seen here: namely, to limit freedom through social control. Externally, the state must protect its citizens form foreign invasion. Internally, the state must create a stable social order. No social order may exist in which every individual can do whatever he pleases. This would constitute anarchy. Whatever freedom is granted must be in relation to the establishment and maintenance of social order. 'Power to the people' means nothing in this regard. The people once had power. They call it the Paleolithic Age!

14. "Reason is developmental and needs the discipline of authority to direct it."

Commentary: Since the Enlightenment, there has been a rebellion against tradition and authority. Of course, there were rebellions before that, yet they now take on an intensity which is destructive. There is nothing more dysfunctional than a rebel! Most rebels want to destroy, but have little idea of what should follow after the apocalypse. The French revolutionaries wanted to create utopia, yet unveiled a monstrous, vile reign of terror! Tradition often embodies

169

deep structures of wisdom established through the ages which should not be arbitrarily disregarded and reason needs authority to direct it or control its functions..

'My being' is enveloped in a "lived body". It receives sensations which, through bodily interpretation, lead to ideas being formed by the mind or the rational faculty. Those sensations could be external or internal as in the case of memories. The resulting ideas, however, are not representational and are in no manner a copy of the real. They constitute 'my world' which is not necessarily 'your world'. Authority must, therefore, through the internalization of language or culture, social structure or institutionalization, create the functional imperative of a 'common world' which is a world of little more than authoritative subjugation. Without authority there is no common world.

One more word is necessary. The cognitive capacity is both active and passive. It may be intentional, yet at times may be inert. Enveloped in bodily activity, a mental notion is formed, but is only in part conscious. Moreover, there are potentialities inherent at birth which may be common to all humanity, but may also be unique to specific individuals. That is, to no other man!

15. "Being is embodied in man's individual finiteness".

Commentary: Being is enveloped in man's individual finiteness. Being-in-itself is nothing. The Ancient Greeks were mistaken in their quest to capture the essence of the ground of Being. We may reach for Being, yet may never touch it. It is only 'my being' which may be discerned, yet it is discerned within the tyranny of space and time. In Kantian terms, space as the tyrant of the external and time the despot of the internal. Thus, all categories are phenomenal categories. Metaphysical categories may be beyond time and space. All that is left is 'my being'.

'My being' is existential- it is a deed-act derived from my concrete self. It is finite, singular, semi-isolated, indeed, autobiographical and produces the notion of 'my world' which is a unique vision or an exit, a limited solipsism. Abstract, universal solipsism is absurd since the world is in me and I am in the world. But, as a psychological-logical argument, not to be confused with traditional logic, 'my world' is all that is since I can never prove that 'my world' is equivalent in content to any other man's world. Thus, this is an exit from the notion of a common world.

There is no universal principle to be revealed in the investigation of 'my being'. Heidegger studied the concrete being of the individual, yet seemed to believe that there were universal principles to be derived from such an investigation. This claim is denied here as there is no such thing as human being as a generic notation. But, more than this. Heidegger seemed to believe that the investigation of being in the life-world uncovers the nature of Being-in-Itself as the ultimate metaphysical category. The truth is that the concrete can never touch the base of divinity.

Husserl also conceived of phenomenology as revealing a universal insight: namely, to be the most rigorous and justified science of investigation. It is a significant descriptive method, yet its principles are modified here. Phenomenology must be autobiographical in its revealing and biographical in its reception. Whether the world is 'in here' or 'out there' is irrelevant. The point is that the world is in me and I am in the world. Doubt is fine and we may retain certain terms as metaphors, but there is no universal essence of anything in general or even of 'my being' in particular as that being may change during the temporal process. In addition, there is the great limitation: namely, finitude.

Finitude is a hole in the fabric of all optimism. Man has limited strength, limited intellect, limited foresight, limited empathy and limited survival potential. Finitude envelops him. A man is born on a single day and dies on a specific day. I say day because men do not conceive of their death as happening on a singular day. They will die somewhere in the future, the remote future, no doubt-years, decades or during some month in that interval. But, to die on a day, that is concrete and reveals the horrid reality of death. Why must I die? This might be the beginning of philosophy as it gives an initial stimulus to the sensitive mind.

16. 'As Heidegger wrote, we are 'thrown' into an already existing world of social facts.'

Commentary: There is no plan for our existence. We are 'thrown' into this miserable world of social facts which stands apart from us and constrains our behavior. It is a social 'a priori' and in no way is it universal as everyone internalizes the cultural and social order differently. We become human through the internalization of those social standards. The social order is, in Max Weber's terms, an 'iron cage' limiting our freedom and the 'my being' of each individual rebels against this ascribed constraint. Hence, the desire to 'throw back' into the face of being our resentment at this existential tyranny. From this comes nihilism, the hatred of God, of life itself and of society: This is the true 'death instinct'. It is possible that what is 'thrown back' is love and compassion, yet this would arise from empathy for the general misery of mankind. What we 'throw back' is our interpretation of meaning.

17. 'Prior to socialization, 'my being' knows no ethics, no law, no logic...'

Commentary: We only have potential at birth- potential which will never be realized without socialization or the learning process about the social world. Here we learn language or the repository of all symbolic meanings and from this we internalize values, folkways, mores and laws. Without this, there is no civilized behavior. The divine has not imposed it from above. Thus, the state must mandate sanctions, both positive and negative.

18. 'Truth is embodied in 'my being' as 'my being' is my truth.'

Commentary: This view has antecedents in the philosophy of both Thomas Aquinas and Martin Heidegger. In Aquinas' philosophy, truth relates to being and has viability only in relation to that concept. To Heidegger, truth is a revealing or unveiling of being, not a matter of propositional affirmation.

Chapter 3

19. 'All philosophy is theoretical and remains so no matter what efforts are made to render it practical.'

Commentary: Philosophy is theoretical. It can never have the preciseness of science or the practical concreteness of ethics. No one invents their own ethical system as no one invents their own language. Both are social facts and are above the individual in the sense that they exercise an external constraint. No invented system of ethics, either Kant's or Mill's, can regulate a person's behavior for the good and sufficient reason that the superego represents the internalization of society's mores, not the individual's private ethical preferences. With the exception of the titans, that superego will bind you to moral worth.

20. 'Man is more than a stream of categories, but a presence, a deed-act, a biographical singularity and a component in the fabric of total comprehension.'

Commentary: Man is no more than a component in the totality. His finiteness prevents any comprehension of the infinite. In this sense,

Nicholas of Cusa is correct in that there is a wall between the finite and the infinite through which we may never pass. 'My being' is beyond all objective analysis. Hence, the need for faith and inwardness.

The more I reflect, I become more convinced that the father of existentialism was correct in that there are two ways to think of God: namely, the objective and the subjective. The objective will never reveal God. No one comes to God through the intellect. It is only the inward path of faith and subjectivity which might touch the base of the divine. Yet, it is the inner truth of 'my being', not just the relationship, which is the key. Being can only relate to Being.

21. 'Unlike poetry or literary genre, philosophy must meet the test of critical discussion, contradictory evidence and rebuttal.'

Commentary: Much of philosophy does, yet the metaphysics of 'my being' need not. My truth is èternal. It is the record of a vision, not to be touched by any profane hand. Contradiction is irrelevant to 'my being' which is embodied in contradictions. Life is not an equation, but an embodied deed-act. Heidegger was wrong. Metaphysics is not the study of Being, but rather the study of the subjective nature of 'my being'. He examines this only in terms of revealing universal structures of existence. This claim is denied here. 'My being' is a singularity and in no way reveals the nature of Being itself. Hence, metaphysics relates to my truth: namely, I am.

22. 'Thus, the continual necessity to invent new words...'

Commentary: Language is a mechanism of survival and its pragmatic nature is a barrier to truth. Our thinking is inhibited by the structure of language which is, after all, one of Wittgenstein's basic insights. This is specifically true in relation to the subject-predicate structure of language. Husserl stresses the subject more. Merleau-

Ponty focuses more on the object. Other philosophers discuss the relationship between the two. Thus, language is structuring our thought and new words are needed in order for novel conjectures to be realized. Perhaps, reality transcends this subject-predicate format.

'My being' knows no such bifurcation. 'My being' and 'my world' are one. Neither is 'in here' or 'out there'. This is simply an artificial distinction of language. It should be noted that both Bradley and Whitehead reject all such dualisms.

This is actually one of the non-motivational functions of art: that is, those that go beyond any expressive purpose, but rather pertain to the entire human condition. Art is a non-grammatical means of transcending the formality or grammatical structure of written or spoken language. Art is not subject-predicate bound and its symbols are malleable in that they represent an aesthetic idea which transcends and envelops the limits of language.

Chapter 5

23. 'We attack being-itself in revenge for our own finitude'

Commentary: We form an idea of the ground of being and resent its infinity given our finite nature. We are, in Heidegger's words, a 'being on to death'. Our termination is always ahead of us and we resent it. We wish the earth under us would shake and we could rise to the sky. Yet, the dust is our fate. As Napoleon stated, there is no immortality except the memory we leave in the minds of men. Hence, the necessity to 'throw back' into the core of being the meaning of our existence. Having been 'thrown in', it is in the nature of retribution that we should 'throw back'. This is existential justice. As Anaximander noted, there is a penalty for being. Yet, we resent it.

Chapter 8

24. 'The event is real.'

Commentary: This must not be interpreted in Whitehead's sense since he defines reality in terms of categories. But, 'my being' transcends categories. The event to 'my being' is the process of interaction in 'my world' which leads to a continual stream of ideas, both conscious and unconscious, that motivates action in the 'life-world'

25. 'Most philosophers concentrate on the consequences of moral precepts and ignore the concrete past or present interactions which may dictate any moral choice.'

Commentary: The past is as significant in forming moral decisions as are future consequences. In addition, the concrete as well as the general must be examined. This is the great defect of utilitarianism which examines the past in terms of general rules or formulas which will generate the greatest good for the greatest number in the future. They deal in the general whereas the concrete is what is significant. Instrumentalism is worse. It negates the past in its empirical formulations except in terms of developing a specific hypothesis to solve a problem in the future. To them, the future is the key. The deontologist concentrates on the objective sense of duty devoid of time sequences. Yet, process is the key to ethics as there is no such thing as a static moral decision.

Let me provide an example from history. Sometimes one can understand things better in a famous situation than in a relatively unknown one. Hitler was granted his demands at the Munich Conference in 1938. The English and French were interested in maintaining the peace which is generally a sound goal especially if one considers the massive destruction in the First World War. Yet, the future consequence of maintaining the peace was not more important than examining the past: namely, Hitler's past actions. Considering his murders and policies of destruction, this was not a man who could be trusted. He had boasted that when you lie, tell big lies. Hence, the past negated the future in this case and this was certainly not a proper moral decision. Of course, statecraft rarely empowers morality in its policies which is one of the reasons the world is in such a benighted state. No doubt, in other concrete situations, perhaps maintaining the peace would be more important. The past must be consulted.

Chapter 9

26. "In the end, in a non-verbal, almost transcendent manner, music touches the inner nature of our being or uniqueness."

Commentary: Music is a language in itself, but one which frees us from conventional English, German, Spanish or for that fact any other. It penetrates deep into the nature of every singular individual's 'my being'. It frees us, that is, from conventional grammar which is a wall of obstruction blinding us from our true nature. We fall silent in the face of grave sorrow. We cannot speak. But, we can feel and there lies the value of music. Connecting feelings with ideas beyond the tyranny of language. You may write about the horrors of World War 2, but Shostakovich's *String Quartet No.3 in F Major* conveys the horror to its zenith, especially in its fifth movement. You feel the pain and the weight of sorrow directly here. It is not a shadow, but a ground of 'my being'. It speaks to something much deeper than the intellect.

27. 'The law prevents deviance by its presence'.

Civil order, of course, deals with more than upholding law. It also incudes the provision of the basic economic necessities as no society can have a proper civic order where large segments of the population exist in a state of economic penury.

Outside of the above stated reasons, revolution is not justified. Without the state, every individual's 'my being' would be uncontrolled and the result would be anarchy quite similar to Hobbes' hypothetical state of nature. A temporary dissatisfaction with public policy is not a proper justification.

There is no implication here that the state arose as a result of a contractual agreement for mutual protection, but rather by a continuous cultural and social structural evolution necessitating its formation by hierarchy, tradition or conflict.

Culture generates the state, not power which is one of its functions.

Appendix 2 - The Apocalypse

This historical novella, published in 2004, provides a fictional format for many of the ideas expressed in this text. It provides a phenomenological description of one singular individual's conscious recollections. It ties the concrete with the general and the personal with the historical. It suggests that profound philosophical problems have meaning not in terms of generalities, but only in the raw flesh of concrete experience.

Bertrand Sovare is an intellectual who despises intellectuals. "Intellectuals love books, not people." He is a sensitive man who murders and desires to murder more. He is a man of contradictions. He both loves and hates Adolf Hitler. He is a loyal Nazi, yet is arrested for political crimes against the Reich. He tries to be a good Christian, but bitterly criticizes Christ. His life demonstrates that contradiction is the law of reality, as Hegel suggested.

He is wounded by man, society and nature and desires to strike back. He wishes an asteroid would hit the earth. He wants to 'throw back' vomit into the web of life. He is in rebellion against being-itself, whatever that phrase means. He makes it clear that his world is not your world and his humanity is not yours. Vomit is his ethics.

Does God exist? Why is there evil? What is the ultimate good? These are not abstractions to him, but the blood of his being. He dreams of utopia, yet justifies murder. What sort of a man is this? Only his phenomenological recall may reveal the answer!

A Selective Bibliography

Alexander, Samuel, *Moral Order and Progress: An Analysis of Ethical Conceptions*, 2nd Edition, London, Kegan, Paul, Trubner & Co., 1891. A now nearly forgotten philosopher, yet important during the early 20th Century. Paul Edwards once said that Alexander attained well-deserved oblivion. The present author disagrees.

Anselm, *Basic Writings*, ed. & trans., by Thomas Williams, Hackett Publishing, IN, 2007.

Anselm's ideas on the proof of God's existence are among the most original in philosophy. Kant labeled it the ontological argument. Almost every major philosopher has since evaluated this attempted proof either positively or negatively including Descartes, Leibniz and Schopenhauer. Anselm's general ideas concerning the nature of being in other parts of his writings invoke intimations of Heidegger's later thinking.

Aristotle, *The Organon*, ed. by Roger Bishop Jones, NY, 2016.

His mind almost proves the existence of a species higher than man. He made contributions to every major field of philosophy, science and literature. His contributions to logic were the essence of the discipline until about 1945.

Aristotle, **Physics**, trans. by Robin Waterfield, Oxford University Press, NY, 2008.

An amazingly complex analysis of the subject for a man who lived in the 5th Century B.C..

Aristotle, **The Basic Works of Aristotle**, ed. by Richard McKeon, Random House, NY, 1941.

This work includes selections of all aspects of Aristotle's writings. The reader should pay particular attention to his ideas on metaphysics. Aristotle's conception of god is truly novel and has influenced scores of later thinkers including Whitehead and McEwen.

Augustine, Saint, *Saint* Augustine's *Confessions*, trans. by Henry Chadwick, Oxford University Press, 1991.

This is exactly the sort of first-person analysis which is needed in philosophy. A classic for all ages.

Ayer, A. J., *Language, Truth and Logic*, Dover Publications, NY, 1952,

A classic presentation of the logical positivist position including the famous verification principle. Naïve, but remember that it is the work of a philosopher who was not yet thirty years of age.

Burnet, John, *Early Greek Philosophy*, London & Edinburgh, Adam and Charles Black, 1892.

An important work on the pre-Socratic philosophers. Extremely well-researched and thoughtful. The reader should pay particular attention to the chapters on Héraclitus and Parmenides.

Berger, Peter, & Luckmann, Thomas, *The Social Construction of Reality: A Treatise on the Sociology of Knowledge*, Anchor Books, NY, 1966.

An insightful argument maintaining that the human world surrounding us is socially constructed and maintained by symbolic universes of meaning. Man externalizes his own world which then stands extraneous to him as a social fact which in turn is internalized by the next generation.

Campbell, D., Cook, T., Shadish, W., *Experimental and Quasi-Experimental Designs for Generalized* Causal Reference, Boston, Haughton Mifflin, 2002.

Too bad that the logical positivists could not have read this book. They might have learned about the complexity of social research. In particular, they would have attained a greater awareness of the factors of internal and external validity.

Campbell, Joseph, *The Portable Jung*, Penguin Books, NY, 1976.

A literate collection of the ideas and insights of the inventor of analytic psychotherapy. The reader should pay particular attention to Jung's beliefs about archetypes and the collective unconscious.

Delia, Edward, **The Apocalypse**, Vize Publications, NY, 2004.

A historical novella on the life of Bertrand Sovare, a former Nazi, who is arrested and detained for political crimes. A fictional format constituting a first-person account of philosophy.

Freud, Sigmund, **The Interpretation of Dreams**, trans. & ed. by James Strachey, Basic Books, NY, 2010.

A classic demonstrating that dreams are an alternative thought process. Insightful and stimulating. Later psychotherapists have modified Freud's ideas, yet the essential structure remains untouched.

Heidegger, Martin, **Being and Time,** *trans.* by John Macquarrie, Harper & Row, NY, 2008.

One of the most original philosophers in modern times. His presentation of phenomenology represents a gateway to the original study of the nature of being as advocated by the pre-Socratics.

Husserl, Edmund, *Ideas:* **A General Introduction to Pure Phenomenology, trans.** By R. Boyce Gibson, Routledge, London & NY, 2012.

An important introduction to the art of phenomenology by an esteemed philosopher.

Jaspers, Karl, **Anselm and. Nicholas of Cusa**, ed. by Hannah Arendt, trans, by Ralph Mannheim, Harcourt, Brace & Jovanovach, NY & London, 1966.

An intelligent analysis of the philosophies of Anselm and Nicholas of Cusa by a great existentialist. The reader should pay significant attention to how similar Anselm's ideas are to Heidegger's later writing. In addition, Cusa's philosophy is presented and analyzed in its full majesty.

Kant, Immanuel, **Critique of Pure Reason**, ed. Marcus Weigett, Penguin Classics, NY, 2007.

A voyage into the realm of the 'a priori' for those intellectually brave enough to venture. Historically, the book is said to have almost driven a friend of Kant's nearly insane in his attempt to read it all. In 1970, several professors suggested that I read this classic and as a young student, I didn't obey. Much later, I ventured an attempt with some reward and much anxiety. The book, however, must be read for those who seriously study the history of this discipline.

Lewis, C. I., **Mind and the World Order: Outline of a Theory of Knowledge**, Dover Reprint, NY, 1956.

A classic in epistemology establishing the notion of the pragmatic 'a priori' in philosophy. This is, no doubt, the best of Lewis' writing and his ideas are truly original.

Merleau-Ponty, Maurice, **The Phenomenology of Perception,** trans. Donald Landes, Routledge, NY & London, 2012.

An essential classic in phenomenology by a great French phenomenologist. A work of genius. Difficult, yet worth the effort to attain a relatively self-determined understanding of the issues.

McEwen, William, *Enduring Satisfaction,* The Philosophical Library, NY, 1949.

An interpretation of philosophy by a student of Whitehead who had his doctoral dissertation supervised by Whitehead. A great book to learn about Whitehead's ideas, yet it is more than that. McEwen goes on to present his own philosophy of existence. The reader should pay particular attention to McEwen's ideas on God and the good life.

Plato, **The Republic**, Benjamin Howett, trans. Heritage Illustrated Publishing, 2014.

The most essential and influential classic in philosophy. Whitehead was correct when he observed that all philosophy is a series of footnotes to Plato. The reader should pay specific attention to Plato's ideas on justice.

Whitehead, Alfred, N., **Process and Reality**, The Free Press, NY, 1979.

A grand vision of a metaphysical system by a master of process philosophy. Essential for serious students of metaphysics.

Wittgenstein, Ludwig, **Tractatus Logico-Philosophicus**, trans. by C.K. Ogden, Dover, NY, 1999.

A classic attempt to provide an 'a priori' proof of a picture theory of language. Wittgenstein rejected it in subsequent writings, yet it is still worth a good effort toward the goal of insight.

A Selective Glossary

Absolute- That which is independent of or unconditioned by anything else. Aristotle's conception concept of god or Spinoza's idea of substance would be prime examples.

Analytic Philosophy- a 20th century movement which believes that philosophical issues are primarily those pertaining to language. A.J. Ayer would be a prime example of this type of philosopher.

A posteriori- Knowledge which is derived from experience. Join Locke's thinking fits this pattern.

A priori- Knowledge which is prior to or independent of experience. Kant is the main exponent of the 'a priori' in epistemology, ethics and aesthetics. Otto believed that the holy is an 'a priori' category and Chomsky advocated an 'a priori' theory of language development.

Archetype- The ideal pattern, form or model representing an existing or imaginary entity. Jung and Joseph Campbell believed that archetypes are transmitted from one generation to another through the genes as found in dreams and mythology.

Being-That which is or is recognized as existing. The fundamental question of metaphysics is to explain what is, what ought to be and the nature of the universe as a whole. Parmenides essential question concerns what is and Heidegger later expanded the inquiry into what it is to be a human being. Philosophy begins with the concept of being and ends there. Being is itself is the tautology of tautologies, yet a significant tautology.

Categorical Imperative- Immanuel Kant's fundamental principle of morality. Act so the maxim of your action becomes a universal law of nature. As with all generalizations it has limited utility.

Causality- Every effect must have a sufficient cause responsible for its existence. Hume demonstrated that the principle is unprovable.

Cosmos- This concept derives from the early Greeks and it posits an unfounded belief that the universe is predictable and orderly. Based on the limited observation and reasoning of one species in a tiny corner of the universe, it is no more than an unprovable axiom.

Doubt-This concept is probably the beginning of wisdom and it posits a gap or uncertainty in response to any proposition. Hume has been called the great skeptic and Montaigne is not far behind in this regard.

Epistemology- A sub-discipline in philosophy which examines the nature of knowledge and the conditions under which knowledge may be posited. C.I. Lewis is a great epistemologist as was David Hume.

Ethics- A sub-discipline in philosophy concerned with two essential questions. First, what is the highest good? Second, how ought we to act? Other queries may be considered, yet these two are the most fundamental. In the 20th Century, the question of ethical language has been deemed to be paramount.

Existentialism- A method of thinking in philosophy which concentrates on man's concrete existence and such issues as alienation, freedom, ethical choice and man's relationship to the divine. Jaspers and Heidegger are great existentialists.

Foundational Truths- An ill-conceived belief that all knowledge is based on a few rationally provable first principles. Descartes began the modern quest and has had many followers. This is a form of philosophical alchemy as first principles are themselves unprovable.

Idealism- The philosophical belief that the ontology of the world consists of nothing except ideas.

Bishop Berkeley would be the prime example of this type of thinking. He denied the existence of of material causes maintaining that there are only minds, ideas and notions. Schopenhauer presented a different version of idealism maintaining that our knowledge of the world consists of nothing except ideas, yet the ontology of the world manifests an uncaused, timeless, all-pervasive Will.

Indeterminism-The belief that there are actions or behaviors which are uncaused or free of determination. This view is to be contrasted with determinism which maintains that all events are causally determined. Both beliefs retain some truth which is resolved by the conception of relative self-determinism as advocated by McEwen and Whitehead.

Infinity- One of the more important concepts in philosophy. It posits an endless progression of time or events in space-time. There will be no limit or boundary here. Man's finiteness cannot grasp infinity.

This was the fundamental insight of Nicholas of Cusa who posited a wall between the finite and the infinite. The infinity of time and space in itself bars any final conclusions in science. Man must limit himself to his finite reality.

Innate ideas- The belief that some ideas are not founded upon experience nor upon rational reflection. To the contrary, they are inborn or, as Descartes would assert, derived from God and their reality serves as evidence of his existence. Jung and Joseph Campbell both advocate the reality of innate notions.

Metaphysics- The study of what is, what ought to be and the nature of the universe as a whole. In. ontology, the study of the nature of being. Spinoza, Aristotle and Schopenhauer were great metaphysicians as was Plato.

Nihilism-The belief that life is meaningless and that nothingness will ultimately prevail.

Schopenhauer at times seems to be a nihilist, yet he really was not finding-value or significance in philosophy and music in addition to his belief that the will in nature is indestructible.

Nothing- That which is not. Parmenides maintained that only being is and nothing is inconceivable.

Schopenhauer believed that the world devoid of Will is nothing: Heidegger could not relate the nothing to the Christian conception of God. Nothingness to many individuals is a source of terror. The status of nothingness is a prime consideration in any metaphysical system particularly in relation to the notion of being.

Ontological Argument- Anselm's proof of God's existence maintaining that God's perfect being necessitates his existence. Schopenhauer called it a charming joke. Descartes used a version of it in his thinking as did Leibniz. Kant believed that all other proofs of God's existence are based upon it.

An existentialist noted that no one ever gave their life to defend this proof.

Ontology- The study of being or, in our sense, 'my being'.. Being is the key concept of metaphysics. Phenomenology- In Husserl's terms, a method of investigation concerning the essence of phenomena.

To Heidegger's mind, a method of opening the way to an investigation of being.

Philosophy- The meaning of philosophy is the major problem of philosophy. The reader should consult the text for the details.

Pragmatism- A theory that a proposition must be evaluated in terms of its 'cash value' or practical consequences. Charles Sanders Peirce and William James offer quite different interpretations of this approach.

Rationalism- A method in epistemology which stresses the exercise of reason as the ultimate criterion of truth. Descartes and Spinoza would be the major exponents of this method. The problem remains, however, as to what guarantees reason to the both reliable and valid. What is reason? In the text, some answers are provided.

Realism- A metaphysical view that physical objects exist apart from our representation of them. Not only is this belief unprovable, it is absurd since all we truly know about physical objects is the perception of them as filtered through our bodily reactions.

Solipsism- A belief that only I exist. Absurd, yet possible in terms of logic alone. Hence, the limitations of logic. Social-psychologically, we know that this view is false, yet the ultimate philosophy is me in the sense that my philosophy springs from my being alone. The extensions of that solitary being are merely assumed.

Thomism- A system of thought derived from Thomas Aquinas which stresses the use of faith in addition to reason in solving philosophical queries. Given the limitations of reason, this view is closer to the truth than a strictly rational approach. I think, but I also feel, hope and pray.

Whorfian hypothesis- A belief that the nature or structure of language determines our view of reality. Hence, the dependence of thought upon language. An essential insight to be considered in any philosophical analysis.

About the Author

Edward M. DeLia is a philosopher and social scientist who received his B.A.. Degree from Brooklyn College of the City University of New York in 1970 and graduate degrees from both Hofstra and Fordham Universities in 1977 and 1983. He authored, *The Apocalypse: Historical Fiction on the Third Reich,* which was published in 2004 and believes that great writing must inspire one to think about philosophical issues in a fashion which is clear, powerful and memorable. The son of Edward Delia. Sr, an executive, he has been analyzing philosophical problems for half a century.

BACK COVER

The purpose of this work is to analyze the meaning of philosophy in addition to providing a creative interpretation of the nature of the field. The work begins by positing two essential preconditions which gave rise to the discipline and the reasons why the meaning of the field is not agreed upon by philosophers. A proposed definition is then ventured, yet with no claim of finality. Alternative definitions of philosophy are then given and analyzed.

Next, the value of philosophy itself is explored and its uniqueness. The relation of philosophy to other fields of inquiry are then investigated including religion, mythology, the sciences and the humanities. This includes the necessary training for philosophical insight, the nature of journals in philosophy and the quality of reference books in the discipline. The stratification structure in philosophy is also explored.

The metaphysics of knowledge is analyzed which includes recommendations for future research. The procedure stressed for investigation is then exemplified in the subdisciplines of aesthetics, ethics and philosophy of religion. The book deals with the insights of numerous philosophers and has hundreds of footnotes. A bibliography and glossary are included.

9 798901 810361